Do You.

The Audacity to Live
a Bold and Authentic Life

Dr. Carter —
You see so much
in others. I'm glad
I get to see so much
in you. Keep doing you!

—Sheleah
Reed

Sheleah D. Reed

Published by: Book SIL LLC

Cover Design: Molly Murphy

ISBN: 978-1-387-48685-4

Printed in USA by Lulu.com

Dedication

CONTENTS

ACKNOWLEDGEMENTS

While many of you reading this may be surprised that I was able to write a book at this point in my life (*life has definitely been lifeing*), I'd guess most of you aren't really surprised to be reading a book written by me. Well, I'm surprised that I had the self discipline to make it happen and the audacity to write it all out, along with the gall to be edited (*hey Doc, Sil and Teddy*). More than anything, I have developed the stamina to speak about what I wrote, with those of you who decide to read this book.

There's no way that this book would be possible without Sharon. My mother is all things and she's the one to get it done no matter what. She's superwoman. She's Mimi/GiGi. She's what Martha Stewart wished she was. I can call my mama and tell her anything and she will listen and then give me constructive criticism. She hates all my haters and loves them when she sees them. She keeps all my secrets and reminds me that I can be better while also telling me that I'm perfect. I wrote this book without her knowing, and the whole time I kept thinking...she's going to kill me for keeping her in the dark. Thank you mama for being all things! I'm blessed because I have the absolute best.

I have the best family, too. Buggy is literally the man. He knows all people and by default they know me and my business. He's the perfect wingman. He can show up anywhere and will be himself. Dad, I thank you for passing that trait on to both me and Alden. He is truly your grandson. I appreciate Wyvette for keeping you in line.

My brother is my biggest cheerleader even when he doesn't know how to cheer. Thank you for reminding me to shine, no matter what. Danae, I didn't hear this in your vows but this is what you married into. We all shine when one of us shines.

Those three people are my foundation, but I have a tribe of people who keep me grounded and cheer me on. Thank you for praying for me, celebrating for me, answering my texts, calls, and emails. Thanks for understanding my strange way of communicating and seeing me for me.

If I started listing people, I'd be giving out too many secrets, so I won't. I do know that I have an army of people who are ready, at any moment, to go to war. These are people who mention my name in rooms that my feet have not entered yet. These are people who send me books, song lyrics, quotes, and Bible verses. They will tell me when to cut my hair, what colors to wear, and think that my two boys are their sons. My people constantly tag me in silly things and send me memes. They remind me to laugh, live, and love. I do not have a village. It is indeed an army.

In 2008, I was introduced to someone who has the stamina to put up with me every day. If I were him, I would have thrown it all out and walked away. But he can't do that! God gave me to him as an assignment and I am grateful we get to do life together. I love you, Mr. Reed.

INTRODUCTION

Some of these stories are real and some are loosely based on my life. You'll never know which is which and to be honest, I may have forgotten too. My life has been one interesting event after another and many days I ask God, out loud, what he is up to. In the past, I've questioned him with an attitude and even used a tone of frustration. I still interrogate him at times, but now it's usually just a rhetorical question and a chuckle that follows. The difference is that now, I've learned to lean into the beauty of his Grace and Mercy and accept that His Will will always be done.

It has not been easy to always embrace his promises but once I finally let go, my life became a roller coaster ride that's been both amusing and thrilling. I've also learned to remember that everything that happens is a part of a bigger puzzle that I can't see just yet. I also know that the end has already been written. I'll leave you with a spoiler alert: in the end, we win. Those who love God win. No matter how bad this moment seems or how hard the times get, you will win.

The stories within these pages make up the small ways in which I've learned to live boldly, unapologetically, and authentically me. I've learned that the best way to live life is with my chin held high, my eyes straight ahead, and my hands open. I've placed my confidence in God, and I've ultimately stopped trying to help his plan play out.

In this posture, I've been able to see each person and situation I've encountered as another part of my story... an assignment or a chapter. Because of this, my eyes stay open wide enough for me to focus on what is beyond the obvious and look for the lessons in every moment. With my hands open, I've been able to receive more than I've ever imagined while also giving more than I've ever received.

I don't make up Reedisms. Instead, they just appear and someone along my path writes them down or remembers them. Social media has helped me capture them as well. Either way, I've learned that these catchphrases have become reminders and mantras that have positively impacted those whom I've met. They've become parts of speeches I've given, parts of posts on social media, and phrases that come up in conversations. I've added them to t-shirts and have written them in thank you cards that I've sent to friends and colleagues. My Reedisms remind me of different times in my life and apparently, others have found them useful too. I decided to use them in this book as a way to connect all the dots of my story.

This book almost didn't happen. I read, wrote, read, and wrote again. Then, I sat on it. The idea... "don't let perfect be the enemy of good" haunted me until I said yes. I've said yes and now these words are out in the world.

So, I hope you find joy while reading. I also hope that you realize that life presents challenges for us all regardless of race, age, sex, education, background, parents, weight, height, income, and whatever else you can think of. Furthermore, I hope the stories make way for you to see that there's a blessing in every circumstance. I hope you realize that every situation you've been in or will be in is a chance to find the bottom line, reflect, and live boldly.

It Ain't About You.

I'm convinced that social media ruined the world we live in. Well, maybe it didn't ruin it, but it surely came along and changed everything. It is easily a blessing and a curse.

One of the main challenges with social media is that most users are on one extreme, or the other. If you love social media, it is most likely because it helps you to generate ideas; it motivates you to work harder, earn more or eat healthier. There is also a chance that you enjoy it because these platforms allow you to connect with friends, family, and strangers from both near and far.

The other side of the coin — those who dislike social media — usually claim it is because the constant access to others leaves them overwhelmed. I can imagine that there are too many images or some people use social media as a mirror or as a measuring stick to determine if they are hitting the mark or aligning with their generation's social cues. There's a ton of "what you should do next alarms" disguised as notifications and to be honest, it is getting more and more challenging to decipher what is real and what is fake.

I must admit that I've gotten caught in the conundrum of going from one side of the coin to the other, but most days the scale is tipped toward the benefits of social media. I am not a super fan, but I am an active user.

I was on Twitter back when there was a 140-character limit for messages and most people simply shared random facts about their location or what they were doing. The interwebs weren't crowded or flooded. Twitter was mostly a work tool.

I used it to connect with others in my industry and to monitor what was going on across the world. I was using Facebook when it was limited to college students with an email address that ended in .edu. According to my notes, I joined Instagram during its first year in 2010 (*probably to keep up with the cool kids*) and I have a ton of boards on Pinterest. That particular tool helped me to plan all my family portraits, my home re-model, and a few parties.

For me, social media is more good than bad. If someone stops by to see what I posted or com-ments on a photo, then excellent. If not, then that's just what happened. No love lost. I use so-cial media, especially Facebook, to remind myself of what's happening in my life. It is a journal or scrapbook of sorts. I also use it to connect with people who aren't in my original friend circle.

It's also my search tool. If I want to know about someone, I put their name in the search bar and boom, I've learned more about them than you can imagine based on who they are connected to or how they are connected to others. When I need examples or inspiration, I head to Insta-gram. Just by looking up a hashtag, I can discover the latest book to read, the fashion trends, the best Mexican restaurants in just about any city.

The reality is that many people use social media to gauge what's going on in their own life and compare it to others. They are looking at the Kardashians, LeBron James and his (*beautiful*) family, and their high school classmates. They are looking at what is happening in this place or that place and keeping an eye on their exes and enemies. In my opinion, if you are using social media to keep up with the Joneses, you are absolutely setting yourself up. It won't end well.

There are two people with whom I've had intense battles about the use of social media. It always starts with me asking why they are taking a break from social media. We end up in a tango of pros and cons about the benefits of the tools. One of my mentees tells me that he's taking a break from social media because he has FOMO (*fear of missing out*). In his mind, when he's not at the club, the party, the football game or the vacation that his friends are on, he becomes overwhelmed. He simply can't handle that others are having a good time and he's at home or work. To avoid being frustrated, he just gets off ALL the tools completely.

The other person, a family member, tells me the tools are a distraction to reaching a goal. Imagine, this person is working on a major project at work or studying for a certification or even trying to lose weight. Because of a lack of discipline to focus on both the goal and browse socially, this family member logs off, reasonably (*maybe responsibly*); because in his mind there's just no way to balance the two things.

My brother and I have also gone back and forth about the value of social media. If you know anything about him, he's a technology authority. He has the latest phone models, has all the cool apps and his house is technologically smart. The dude was on every social media tool as an early adopter. Before most of us found out there was even an app, he had already explored and, more than likely, was no longer using it. Now that he's older, you wouldn't guess that he had these habits. I celebrate when I see his updates and photos. I legitimately cheered when he shared a new status. Social media would have you believe he's not doing anything. This is so far from the truth. He's living a full life — he's just not posting it.

We vacationed in Paris and while I was sharing photos and checking in (*never live, cause you know safety*) he wasn't doing anything. He had the selfie stick and everything — but no posts. I was confused. Here we are, some young professionals, living our best life abroad and he wasn't sharing. We were celebrating his graduation from graduate school, walking along the canal and interacting with the locals, and he wasn't telling his followers. It was weird to me. His reasoning was that he just didn't want people in his business like that. He went on to add that he didn't want people to think he was bragging. Wait, what? Full stop.

I had been where he was before. I also was careful about what I posted. Everything was very, very curated. I was afraid people would see me as braggadocious or that my complaints were "first world problems." True enough, people were dealing with real life struggles and I was concerned about what color shoes I should pick. Yes, people were managing death, and I was celebrating making it to Friday. I was complaining about going to work and one of my followers was dealing with divorce or depression. I had the audacity to post a picture of me gallivanting around the park and someone following me was trying to figure out how to pay their light bill.

I understood his hesitation, but I also saw another side of the story.

People are watching, that's a given. And yes, some of them are haters who don't want to see you actually live well, but I also felt as though he was missing an opportunity to engage with an entirely different audience. What he, even you and me post, isn't connected to the lives that others are living. Because you are happy, you didn't take all the happiness left. Because you are traveling, you didn't take their seat on the plane. Two things can be true at the same time. In fact, I challenged him to use his posts about Paris as an opportunity to show people what is possible.

Far too often, we live and focus on the negatives when, in fact, the positives are where we should spend our time. I heard a phrase — we tend to focus our energy on the people who don't believe in us and proving them wrong. Instead, we should be using our energy on the people who believe in us. We have to stay focused on the notion that the life we live isn't for us. It is indeed for someone else to see what could be.

All my church notes have this concept in them. Every good and bad situation that happens to us AND how we respond is designed to allow others to see how we have overcome the challenge. But like my brother, it gets hard for me to remember that.

There is no secret that my favorite job was my time at my alma mater. It was a dream job. I could immediately see the benefits of my work. So, when I put in my notice to leave for another gig, I had some buyer's remorse.

I kept thinking that I was abandoning a place where I was able to make an impact on young people. I was part of the culture and was depositing and changing the landscaping of the current generation and future generation that would attend the school. It was a tough few weeks.

Every student who stopped by my office made me cry. A young student whom I hadn't had a chance to get to know told me — you are abandoning us. I was leaving projects undone and to top it all, the last day was a groundbreaking for a new building. I wouldn't be there to see it constructed and then put into use. I was challenged that I would never be a valuable player or key component at another organization in the same way.

In my role, I had helped create memories that would never be forgotten and pushed the organization into homes and spaces where we had never imagined it would be. I'd met amazing people and had grown so much, both professionally and personally.

As I was walking to the car with my last box, I was escorted by a student leader. She said to me that she was excited to see where I was going and my leaving reminded her that there's so much more beyond University Drive.

Talk about it not being about you. In that moment, it was clear that I had a bigger assignment and my next role was connected to paving the way for others. I was going to have a major impact and show that students from my alma mater were equal if not better than others. We couldn't be counted out. At that moment I realized that someone was always watching and could be thinking that they could be an astronaut, working mom, author, teacher, doctor (*sub whatever you want here*) because of you.

That could be lost if you aren't posting or sharing your good and bad.

While social media allows our world to seem so connected, the truth is we all live in our own little boxes. Once we close the blinds, we are dealing with real-life issues and trying to make it day by day. Unfortunately, because we are too afraid to share, none of us are benefiting from the lessons of our neighbors. We've got to stop it.

I've challenged myself to post my successes on social media, and I encourage my friends to do the same. The world needs to know that you are out here winning and succeeding. Share that you got a raise, that you got an A on that test, that your child is on the honor roll. I am asking that you post your weight loss journey. And my God, I live for the first day of school photos and the pictures with Santa.

We have to know that others are watching us (*even beyond the socials*) and they need to know that they too can succeed. I promise you that your life is an inspiration for someone. The people behind you are doing more because of the things you are doing. They are thriving because of the hurdles you've jumped and the challenges you've overcome.

The gift of sharing often leads to the magic of connection.

Becoming a mom was not easy for me. It was a long 10-year journey with a lot of twists and turns. It challenged everything I had and had me questioning one thing after another. The good news is that the struggle isn't how the story ends. I've got two little ones who are perfect. But I can't take my baby, go home and hide him. Nor the journey of being a mother.

So many women are walking the same road and while I was on my trek people came out of the blue to answer my questions and cheer me on. They poured into me, gave me feedback and comforted me when it got tough. Throughout my entire process, there were magnolias everywhere and these Mississippi women answered my questions, poured into me and gave me feedback from my first doctor's visit to the labor room.

As a part of my sharing even just a little of my son's birth story, he is walking around with a whole bunch of aunties and uncles. I can never thank all the women who helped me decide what to put on my registry or prayed over me at my baby shower. Instead, I've tried to share the love forward.

I've created a mom group and these ladies from

Seattle to Fort Worth and all the way to Washington and California are in the group sharing how they feel about new bottles. They are talking about postpartum depression and alerting each other about sales at Carter's. It's beautiful to watch them share and connect. It's the true example of it not being about you. Many of us don't have another place to share what we are feeling, and this safe space in our text messages is our safe haven.

I've realized my trials aren't only for me. Many, many times I've watched how the lessons I've learned have been for the benefit of someone else. I've been able to pass on advice that I've received to someone experiencing exactly what I went through.

I'm positive you have some story, a testimony that can help someone else. I challenge you not to hold on to it. That's the whole point of the life we live. We are always in relationship with one another.

This whole project is a testament to learning how to share my story. I've been successful at managing the balance of sharing just enough to connect and holding on to a few tidbits just for me. Over time, I've evolved my approach and realized that as I've heard others say, your experiences aren't yours to carry. You have to write it down, say it out loud and get it out.

The power of sharing our experiences and being true to ourselves can be a reaffirmation of what we believe and what we have learned. We hold on to something and it grows in our head as something far worse than it really is. You were made by God, and for God, and you must know that or life will never make sense.

You were made by God, and for God, and you must know that or life will never make sense.

I have a mentee who experienced this firsthand. By all accounts, he was a model student. He had great grades, was involved in activities, and seemingly had life figured out. He made one choice that took it all away. His grades took a dive, he went into depression, and lost access to what he had worked so hard to build. It was hard to watch. I watched a young man, who was full of confidence and life, disappear.

He was losing weight. He couldn't put sentences together and was absent from all the places he belonged. The hardest part was that there was not a single action anyone could make to change the situation. Like so many of us, he was living through the consequences of his actions. I'd guess that he was ashamed and hurt.

Out of the blue, one day, he showed up with his head held high.

I asked what happened to cut the light back on and he explained that he realized he had to tell his story to others. Because he was a leader and an example to his peers, he felt that he had to share with others how his decision-making impacted him. And it had to be done out loud.

It was a moment of clarity for him. His "story" — both his lowest and proudest moment — wasn't over but the chapter he was living through was coming to a close and was the perfect opportunity for him to demonstrate to others how to overcome challenges. He was disciplined to stay in his mess AND clean it up. That moment changed him. He realized something that takes many people years to learn: being confronted by the realities that come with sharing negative and even triggering experiences can turn into growth.

Since then, I've watched him blossom into someone who is actively aware of his actions and how they are connected to his assignment from God. That change has not caused him to live his life with the blinds closed, rather he is often sharing his thoughts, posting his wins and his losses. He's made decisions that force people to ask him about his choices. He's bolder about who he is and what he is interested in.

We have a relationship that allows me to know more about him than what he posts to social media, but I am so glad he uses his accounts to share. There are hidden gems, sermonettes, and valuable lessons in his comments, in his photos, and in his journey. I can't imagine the number of people who have been blessed and impacted by his 140 (*or so*) characters.

The Bottom Line.

It's not about you. The life you have is designed to be an inspiration for someone else. Because of the trees you are planting, people behind you will benefit from the shade.

A Little More.

If you aren't telling your story, then others won't know when and how to cheer for you. While it is easy not to share due to fear of judgment, sharing the struggle, the pain, the beauty, and the triumph may be the thing that will help someone else win their own race. We should all be willing to share how we got to our positions and the lessons that we learned along the way. Storytelling gives us a great and more whole experience of life. Once a story is told, it becomes a shared experience, one that becomes part of all of us. It causes everyone who is listening to reflect on our words. It could even lead to others having the courage to share their stories, too.

Your Turn.

- What is stopping you from telling your story?

- What shame do you have?

- What are the worst and best things that could happen?

- If you shared, whose life might you impact?

_____

_____

_____

_____

_____

_____

_____

_____

_____

_____

_____

_____

_____

_____

_____

_____

_____

_____

_____

_____

_____

_____

_____

_____

_____

_____

_____

_____

_____

_____

_____

_____

_____

_____

_____

_____

_____

_____

_____

_____

_____

_____

_____

_____

_____

_____

_____

_____

_____

_____

_____

_____

_____

_____

_____

_____

_____

_____

_____

_____

_____

Life is Complicated.

When you are born with a multi-syllable name like Sheleah, you learn quickly that there are two choices in life: be the person who allows people to mispronounce your name or be the person who reminds people over and over how your mother expected your name to be announced. The latter usually means using the phonetic spelling, sounding it out, and breaking the name down into easy-to-swallow, bite-sized pieces.

Decision time comes swiftly. Usually around the time you have learned to pronounce your name, you've made a decision. And by the time adults are asking your name, you know which choice you will make for the rest of your life.

My name is seven-letters and three syllables and I have been correcting people for a long time. In fact, I'm pretty positive that I did it both loudly and proudly as a toddler. I know I did it as an elementary student and I've corrected my share of people as an adult.

As a kindergartner, I attended a school filled with little pig-tailed, brown-skin girls like me and I joined a crowd of like-minded little ladies who were balancing saying their names correctly while sounding them out as they wrote the let-ters on the top of their paper. My kindergarten class in the early 80s was filled with Tamikas (*TaMika, Tamica*), Kieshas (*Kysha, Kesha*), LaToyas and Kenishas. Complicated and multi-syllable names were plenty.

My mom tells a story of what I now believe was a turning point in my name journey. Third grade. We were new to the neighborhood. My parents moved to a suburban neighborhood and took their two little ones to the local school. Back then, the school was filled with Ashleys, Jennifers and Johns. There may have even been a few Davids. Either way, there was no me. Very few young ladies in my class were balancing the unspoken rule of pronouncing your name for others repeatedly while learning how to spell it correctly yourself. I'm pretty sure I didn't know what a phonetic spelling even was.

When mom picked me up after school one day, the teacher mentioned to her that I probably needed my hearing checked because she'd been calling my name all day and I was not responding. She went into more detail, explaining the importance of hearing and how it could impact my learning and ultimately my place in life.

Now, my mom has been an overachiever her entire life. Class valedictorian, cheer captain, child entrepreneur. There's no way possible that her child — the one she took to the dentist, the optometrist and the hair stylist, and sewed perfect school outfits for — had hearing issues. It was impossible that she didn't know I allegedly had hearing issues before that day.

When she tells me the story now, I always imagine that she looked around as the teacher finished her statement to confirm she was talking to her because there was no way possible she was talking about her child, Sheleah. I was pretty talkative, the kind who held conversations with adults. Yes, the kind who came home with conduct issues because I wasn't able to keep quiet while the teacher was talking. I also didn't quite understand the concept of giving others the chance to answer the question if I knew the answer. For the record, I'm still working on this.

The teacher explained to mom that she called roll and I didn't answer when she got to my name. Her worry and concern continued as she explained that she came to my desk and asked how I was doing. Apparently, I didn't respond.

My guess is that I smiled and grinned at her, more concerned about her and her strange actions. Sugar and spice and all things nice is what they say about little girls. For me, it was heavy on the spice. There was lots of concern for others as my parents and family raised us with the safety net of support and the reminder that others may also need help and support. It was up to us to show compassion and empathy at all times.

Once the teacher finished her story, mom immediately called my name and waved me over. She asked if I had been ignoring the teacher.

Me: no. (*Maybe, I said no ma'am. I'm not sure.*)

Here's where it gets tricky. I think we gathered our belongings and went home. I don't remember anything different happening that evening and I surely don't recall going to the doctor or having my hearing checked. She may have cleaned them after I finished bathing, but that's about it.

The next day, I saw my mom talking with the teacher, though. We got there a tad bit early and while I went to put my lunch kit in my cubby; they were engaged in conversation. Mom did most of the talking. For the rest of the year, whenever the teacher addressed me, I heard her loud and clear.

I'm positive she learned how to accurately say the syllables of my name in correct order and my guess is that mom explained that I only respond when I'm addressed directly and correctly.

That teacher hasn't been the last person to call me by someone else's name or to say my name incorrectly. In fact, it happens pretty consistently.

When you have a full name, it comes with the territory. Having a full name and a mom who has the audacity to name you that way, and the power to provide you the space to grow into your name, is a gift. Yet, it's not a gift that's always something you treasure.

This gift makes life complicated. There's a balance between understanding that your full self will be something like your name — mispronounced and misunderstood — and it's up to you to make it easy to say or help people handle it. You also have the choice to walk away from it all together and give people the chance to choke on it all or to power through and chew on it.

Having a full name and a mom who has the audacity to name you that way, and the power to provide you the space to grow into your name, is a gift. Yet, it's not a gift that's always something you treasure.

I have not figured out the balance. There are situations in which I want my name pronounced correctly — by my doctor's nurse, the name-caller at graduation, the customer service agent on the phone. In these moments when it is announced wrong, I stop, correct the person and even give them tips on how to say it. Yep, I am using the phonetic spelling, sharing rhyming words, and breaking down the story of Leah in the bible. We usually go further into me not having a nickname and how my mom didn't have an actual story around the origin of my name. I've commented that Spanish speakers usually say my name perfectly and I recount the number of people I know with the same spelling. Right now, it's two.

Then there are other times when I don't seem to be bothered. For example, at the bank (*just cash my check please*) or the grocery store (*insert fake smile as the cashier is looking at my debit card, trying to sound it out*). For the record, there's been a person in every single workplace I will not correct. Not because I'm afraid, but because I've corrected them once — usually a few times after our initial introduction.

Why I don't correct them is where it gets complicated. In my opinion, I've done my work — said my name, spelled it out, heard others give tips and now I've decided that apparently they don't have a good understanding or have determined that the correct pronunciation of my name is not worth learning. In either case, they have self-selected their place on my priority list and, as a result, I have moved on. See the story above about my third-grade teacher.

Usually, others ask me why I don't correct them. I've never come up with a good, solid response. It has been easy enough to say — it's complicated. Life is complicated.

What I have decided is that if I correct them, I am spending time on something that doesn't matter to them, so ultimately I'm wasting time I could spend on something else. You are probably thinking, "If that was me, I'd be correcting them every single time." I want to take a moment, though, to challenge you to think about what you have decided to ignore before for the sake of your peace and your sanity? What are you deciding to ignore to simply live? It's complicated, huh? Told you.

To throw a monkey wrench in, I married a man whose name is constantly mispronounced — by the way, it's pretty simple and very common. Then, I had the audacity to give both of my kids uncommon names. I've decided to always correct people when they mispronounce either name, which complicates things even more.

The Bottom Line.

Everything isn't black or white. There's a lot of gray. There's an opportunity to decide and then change your mind. There's no reason to think it's concrete. You can also choose the hard thing and decide that it's just never going to be easy. Life is absolutely complicated, but you get to decide when you want it to be.

A Little More.

We often believe that when we make a decision about something, we are committing to it. I'd challenge that we have the chance to make a decision and once we learn more, decide to feel differently and experience something else. We can absolutely abort the mission and change courses. We aren't stuck in our boxes and don't have to live with our decision. I started by telling you that I ignored someone because they didn't say my name correctly and I'm ending by telling you that I make a decision about who I ignore and who I correct. It is not the same each time. I also purposely decided to give my children names that someone would have to work at. They'd have to decide to say it correctly. It was a decision to accept the difficulty. A decision to make life complicated.

Your Turn.

- Can you pinpoint the places in your life that are complicated?
- What can you do to change that?

_____

_____

_____

_____

_____

_____

_____

_____

_____

_____

_____

_____

_____

_____

_____

_____

_____

_____

_____

_____

_____

_____

_____

_____

_____

_____

_____

_____

_____

_____

_____

_____

_____

_____

_____

_____

_____

_____

_____

_____

Get You Some Cheerleaders.

The day I met her was a normal workday. There was nothing that stood out about it. I do not recall the day of the week. I can't even recall the weather or exactly why she walked into the office. It was simply a normal workday. However, what she did that day was what stood out.

She walked up to me, looked me in the eye, extended her hand, and introduced herself. She told me that she previously worked for the same company and that she was stopping by to speak to the staff. She shared with me that she had several friends who also worked there in another department and had heard that I was leaving the company. According to them, she just had to meet me.

We then went into general conversation about the business and eventually parted ways. It was a pleasant exchange.

Over the next week, she returned to the office, as she had been asked, to assist during my transition. She quickly jumped in and offered both her skill set and her time. She took notes, created her own procedures, and developed processes to help her complete the assigned tasks. She took a lot of pressure off me. In the meantime, we talked about what mattered: office gossip, boys, the latest songs and the best restaurants in the city. It was a natural rhythm. Like most people from Houston, we only had a few degrees of separation. She knew people whom I knew and she had been in all the places and spaces that I frequented. We just never crossed paths.

I left that job, and we kept in touch. It has been almost 25 years since she walked into that office, yet she's one of the first people I call with good news. I've written countless recommendation letters for her and I'm always intrigued by what she has going on and where she may be traveling. She's not someone that my mom would know by name and she doesn't get invited to the boys' birthday parties, but that doesn't make her any less of a friend.

In fact, she's a good one.

She's the friend who told me when it was time to leave one of my previous jobs. To be exact, she listed 26 reasons I needed to turn in my letter of resignation. For any of my counterarguments, she had pre-written rebuttals to cancel each one out. Apparently, I had done enough complaining and by her calculations, my time was up.

She asked me when I was moving into a new house after she'd visited my home for the first time. In her opinion, it was handsome and well accommodated, but I had outgrown it. She has me getting a doctoral degree on her bingo card for my life. She's saved some of her travel itineraries because in her opinion, I must see these places before my life is over. She is absolutely a high-frequency friend — she is inspiring and leaves me energized. Everything about her lights me up and we hold great conversations. One of our conversations about scarves lasted almost two hours. I know that there's not that much to discuss regarding a piece of fabric, but we went into details about colors and different fabrics, knits and folds. So much.

This girl is a believer in me. In some ways, more than I am a believer in myself. She knows my style, believes in my dreams and encourages my shenanigans. All this in exchange for brunch once every few years, random text conversations, and a trail of sharing memes back and forth. I don't count the time I failed at hooking her up with a college classmate. Basically, nothing.

Truth is, my life is filled with many people just like her. We don't talk every day and don't get to see each other often, but when we connect, it's like we never missed a step. With each encounter, everything is placed on the table for discussion: money, religion, family, careers, weight, health, sex, and therapy. Nothing is off limits. My people are the kind of people who will make you up your game. These people always bring their A-game, so you have no choice but to bring yours.

Follow me, this is going to all make sense shortly.

The day "Dreamgirls" debuted at the movie theaters, I was there. I planned my entire Thanksgiving dinner around the 10:35 p.m. showing. I took a nap after hosting my family and then I saved leftovers and packed them away for my movie snack. I had the perfect sweats picked out for the famous play as it made its debut on the big screen.

As a member of the Beyoncé fan club, better known as the BeyHive, I needed to see my girl on the screen. She needed redemption from "Goldmember" and that other movie where she was in a choir. I knew that this was going to be a make or break for her.

Well, wouldn't you know that she sang her face off! The movie was perfect. My friend and I chatted throughout the movie, loudly (*and wrongly*) sang the songs, commented on the outfits and hairstyles and were nearly escorted right out the theater for distracting the other patrons.

"Listen," the song Deena, Beyoncé's character, sang as a breakup/goodbye to her husband Curtis is one of my favorites. I still sing it loud and proud every time it is played on the radio or even when it comes up on my playlist. It's filled with such emotion and character.

There are other parts of the movie that stand out to me, but the main plot that sometimes gets overlooked or downplayed will always be the delicate balance between Effie, who is played by Jennifer Hudson, and Deena. Throughout the movie, their roles are in constant conflict. It is evidently because of their position in the group and at other times it's because of Curtis. One could watch and also make assumptions that body weight comes into play and a further stretch would be their skin tone, as one is fair while the other is a bit darker. In the end, there's not one solid factor that keeps them at odds. Everything keeps them apart. That's the whole point of the plot, but it seems to get overshadowed by the record deals and the baggage that comes with that.

As the movie comes to an end, Deena contacts Effie, they reconcile and walk off (*think of a mod-*

el strutting on a runway with her head held high and chest up kind of walk) into the sunset, closer than ever before.

For years, the movie and play have been connected to the Supremes, the all-girl female group that is part of Motown's long list of hit makers. The main discussion was that Diana Ross, who is joined by three other ladies, was the muse for the play. While she was often the lead singer of the group, the drama hit the highway when the group was renamed, Diana Ross and the Supremes. Interestingly, after several years, she left to pursue a solo career. If you follow conspiracy theories, Beyoncé caught the same flack and carried it into Destiny's Child. Her role as the lead singer is said to be the ultimate cause of the group's breakup. Her diva ways also led to LeToya Luckett being replaced by Michelle Williams (*in this version of the story, we don't consider LaTavia*). Rumors emerged that management showed favoritism to Beyoncé and left the others without finances and access to media or other projects.

My guess is that you were caught up in that hype, too. Many of us are fans of good music and the 90s era of pop and R&B continue to be so many people's favorite. I have long cheered for Beyoncé and knew that like Diana, she would be whisked away from Destiny's Child and perform on her own. Let's not forget that the entire "Say My Name" video is built around her. Her voice is the main one on "Bug a Boo" and in the video, guess who has on a hat? HER. If that doesn't tell you she was being primed for a solo career, I don't know what else to tell you.

It really wasn't until "Soldier" that I realized Kelendria "Kelly" Rowland was holding her own in the group and was actually giving Bey a run for her money. She's been on my radar ever since. Kelly has her own kind of swag. She's independent, has a mix of class and ratchetness and is super confident. She's also the person you want in your corner. When you look at interviews, she's smiling hard when everyone else speaks. She's figured out how to exist and thrive in a world that is focused on Beyoncé and her life. Even R&B crooner Tank said that we were all set up to adore Beyoncé and overlooked the way Kelly performed and just how talented she is. He's right — Mama Knowles made the outfits and did her hair and Mathew was the manager. We were sold a dream.

My guess is that Kelly knows her talents but she also knows that her strength is in supporting others. She's the person who is motivating Beyoncé to shine. She's been able to help her balance motherhood and success and is probably the first person to cheer for her when she wins. Her support doesn't stop there. Kelly also proudly and publicly counts LaLa Anthony and Serena Williams in her BFF group.

To be friends with powerhouses like that, you have to have your own level of confidence. You have to know what you bring to the table and understand there's room for everyone and a chance for everyone to win. Without a doubt, she's a high-frequency friend who is there without motives or secret agendas. She has to genuinely care. These are big friends with big jobs and big personas who are in the public's eye constantly. A few of my friends have good, good jobs — nowhere near the level of Serena Williams but public facing and important — and supporting them has been something that I make a conscious effort to do.

While Kelly has had her own fame through acting, recording, and hosting, she has not entered stardom in the same way Beyoncé has. But that has not stopped her from finding her own lane. I am a superfan of all the Christmas movies that feature her. They are the perfect rom-coms. I am not even thinking about Beyoncé and her husband when I am watching them. It's all about Kelly.

We all need a Kelly in our lives. The problem is too many of us are making people who dislike us our friends. We are taking "keep your enemies close" to heart and surrounding ourselves with people who don't want the best for us. We are going to dinner with the people who don't help us make decisions based on our dreams and wishes. We are laughing and joking with people who are competing against us and we are telling our secrets to people who are telling them to others.

We are taking "keep your enemies close" to heart and surrounding ourselves with people who don't want the best for us.

We need people like Kelly who will help us get to

our next level. We need group members who can harmonize with us, match our energy, hold our place in line and remind us that we can do better.

There's a famous line that is often attributed to Oprah: "You can't be friends with someone who wants your life."

Oprah brings the line to life in her relationship with Gayle. It is clear that the two of them operate in their own lane, but in one quick Google search of either name, the other one's name comes right up as one of the options that people also search for. These two ladies have found a way to support each other, rock for each other, and elevate one another. I think Oprah cried her eyes out when Gayle announced she was going to be a grandmother and if you look in the masthead of Oprah's magazine, Gayle has her own assignment. A permanent job.

I've got a few Gayles in my friend circles. I'm also a few Gayles to some Oprahs. Some of those relationships date back years. I'm talking back before kids were even a thought. A few of the relationships are newer and still being developed. What I've learned over time is that support is fluid and relationships truly are tied to a season and a reason. One of my newest friends has reminded me of that time and time again, yet she's only one call away and has advice for any problem in life.

After I had a baby, she whisked into town with the intention of taking care of me. We ended up at a museum, stopped at every food truck we saw and played UNO late into the night. She remembered each one of those activities was something

I had written down that would bring me joy. I wrote the list at her urging on vacation years ago. I have to believe that Gayle has done something similar for Oprah. She's a friend who will offer survival tips before they are even needed.

Having a relationship like the one O and G have requires friends to not only be comfortable with themselves, but confident in their role and be willing to play it to a tee. The public is often celebrating the superstar and their success. The truth is, it took a team of people to help get the superstar to a place of celebration. I learned this firsthand from someone I never would have expected to teach me the lesson.

I've worked out with a few trainers over the years (*yes, I may need to work out with one now but that's not the point*). They are all different and have unique approaches. I've had an angry, aggressive trainer. You know the kind. He walked around with a clipboard and whistle. He counted loud and strong and would threaten me with extra laps if I didn't do something his way. Every time he yelled, I laughed. Our relationship was like oil and water. It wasn't going to last, and we knew it. He did get me in shape for my wedding, though. I give him complete credit for that.

Another trainer tried a different approach. After our initial consultation, he decided I needed personal sessions and couldn't be part of a group. I suspect I needed that much support. My sessions were intense and hard. The 60 minutes went by fast, but each minute was dreadful. He never yelled. In fact, he whispered at times. I saw results quickly and continued to go to my sessions, always wondering if this was really the right use of my time and money. We understood each other, and he got my philosophy — I am not going to do more because you say it. I am only going to go faster or lift more weights because I want to. I was set on the fact that there was not a single person at the gym or on this earth who would motivate me differently. I was and am always competing against myself, not anyone else.

I figured out his approach. He approached working out as much more than the physical. It was really about mind and heart management. If I was late, he'd say take your time. Whenever I got there, he gave me his complete attention. Even if it was for 15 minutes.

One day, he asked me about my job. I went into a bit of detail, explaining the stress of the role and how my phone was constantly ringing or dinging. He listened intently and nodded, all while spotting me and counting out my reps. During our next session, he hit me with:

"Sheleah, you are a champ. All champs have a corner man. I hope you have more than one."

It was part of his session's closing remarks. He had a one liner every session. Some were funny, others were out of left field. This one was one of the few that stuck with me. I've heard the advice that you are the sum part of the five people you spend the most time with. We all know that birds of the same feather flock together and we've been told that iron sharpens iron. I pass those messages on to others, but the one phrase I always say is, "Get You Some Cheerleaders." Or, as the trainer said, get you some corner men.

These are the people who know the talent you have and are willing to cheer for you even when you are up against an opponent that you probably won't beat. Cheerleaders are the group that leads the fans. They tell them what to say and keep them engaged no matter what.

Have you ever been to a football game that was a blowout? Guess who is still cheering? You guessed it, the cheerleaders. Their hands are clapping and their feet are stomping. If they are good cheerleaders, they are also patting the players on their back as they load the bus back home. We need support systems who continue to cheer for us no matter which way the season is going. When you are up, they are right there next to you. When you are down, they are holding the same position. The best cheerleaders are challenging you to do something more and encouraging you too.

We need support systems who continue to cheer for us no matter which way the season is going. When you are up, they are right there next to you. When you are down, they are holding the same position.

While cheerleaders are supporting you, they aren't in the game with you. They have their own roles and responsibilities they need to do. This is the same for you. You are a part of someone else's system. You are someone else's cheerleader.

I've been called the ultimate connect or as the young people say, the plug. People are counting on me to connect them with someone else. I don't exactly know how I got to this place in life, but here we are. Just the other day someone asked me if I knew someone who lived in Rhode Island. The answer was, yes. I've connected people with DJs and photographers, women to their husbands, a party organizer to a chef, a trainer to a new location. I've helped someone find a seamstress and even a statistics tutor. When I meet someone, I am looking to truly connect and find a way to stay connected to them. I want to be part of their support system. To be a cheerleader for them.

I have a former colleague who does this well. One day at work, she came into my office and asked what I was doing after lunch. I looked at the calendar and rattled off the few meetings I had scheduled. She told me to get ready to celebrate because I was getting a promotion. I was used to her bold statements. She made them often. It was her way of speaking things into existence. You know, what we've all been told to do — call the things that are not, as though they were. She walked out of the office humming Kool and the Gang's "Celebration."

Well low and behold, my supervisor called me in at the end of the day and gave me the rundown on upcoming organizational changes. In that list, was my promotion and raise. Back in my office, my coworker was smiling. I didn't know that for weeks she had been planting a seed about my work and explaining how I deserved a higher position, bigger title, and more responsibility. We laugh about it now and she reminds me that we just don't need mentors and colleagues. We need sponsors who know our work and are speaking up for us when we aren't in the room.

While we had a few things in common and could relate on some level, in the end, we were very different people. That's the thing: your circle of support can't be filled with people who are just like you. You need people who aren't on the exact same path that you are following. They may even believe differently from you. Your circle has to be diverse and include people who look like you and those who don't. Those who may challenge your train of thinking, may introduce you to new places and new people. Your group has to be made up of people who add unique perspectives and who are not afraid to call you out. That is what she did and continues to do. We don't work together, but I can count on her to remind me that I am doing a fantastic job and my organization is lucky to have me as a member of the team.

My squad is one of the best around and each person has a role. Some are just friends, others are mentors, coaches and I even have a few sponsors. Their roles can get confusing, but it's like this: a coach listens to you, a mentor advises you, and a sponsor talks about and acts for you. And age doesn't matter. Take the book club for instance. I'd put that group of women against nearly anyone. The level of conversation is amazing. While we are focused on reading books, the discussions that take place when we get together go beyond the plot and book drama. We are celebrating and lifting each other up. I have the audacity to believe that while favor ain't fair, it is transferable. So when anyone from the book club wins, I stand waiting for the next win and, very well, believing it could be my turn.

I have a few group chats that read like novels. One of them has clear instructions on what to do should I pass away. The other has enough information and background on people with whom we could develop our own version of "Young and the Restless".

I have friends who love Beyoncé and others who never quite get the allure of her success. Whether she is selling out shows, releasing new music under the cover of darkness or singing to Curtis — she needs a cheering squad. Thank God for Kelly.

The Bottom Line.

Surround yourself with people who are there for you at all times, who challenge you, support you, but always have your back.

A Little More.

Shout out to all the cheerleaders: the corner men, the therapists, the pastors, the chat groups, the mentors and the trainers. Shout out to the friends that live far away and the ones that have no clue what you do every day. Shout out to the praying grandmas, aunts and mothers. All of the cheerleaders.

Your Turn.

- Who are your cheerleaders?

- Can you clearly remember a time they cheered you into a win?

- Are you on someone's cheer squad?

_____

_____

_____

_____

_____

_____

_____

_____

_____

_____

_____

_____

_____

_____

_____

_____

_____

_____

_____

_____

_____

_____

_____

_____

_____

_____

_____

_____

_____

_____

_____

_____

_____

_____

_____

_____

_____

_____

_____

_____

_____

_____

_____

_____

_____

_____

_____

_____

_____

_____

_____

_____

_____

_____

_____

_____

_____

_____

_____

_____

The Rules Are Fake.

In my house, we play spades. I probably learned how to play somewhere around 8 to 10 years old. My aunt Sandra taught me. In fact, she taught me how to play gin rummy, tunk, pitty pat, speed, and goldfish. I don't know who taught me how to play dominoes, but my family plays that too. Each of the games comes with its own set of rules.

In speed, you can play doubles. That means you can put two cards down at the same time if they are the same number. At the beginning of a dominoes game, you have to lead with big six, which becomes the spinner. The full color joker is the highest card in every card game and I don't care what UNO's official rules are — at my house you keep pulling until you can play.

My husband doesn't play cards. He thinks he's a master domino player. Yes, he has personalized dominoes, a leather case, and talks shit the entire game. It takes 10 points to start the game and he is the person who always keeps score. You pull until you can play and fives simply don't count on the scoreboard. Those are just the rules. The back man always washes the dishes, and you are allowed to stay on the table until you lose. As a result, there have been plenty of picnics and parties where I left him right on that table and he caught a ride home.

I'm still begging someone to teach me bid whist. I haven't been able to pin anyone down just yet. What I do know is that when you lose, you rise and fly right out the back door. I don't know what that means and I've never seen it, but it seems serious. Everyone I've asked listed it as a rule, so I guess it stands.

I looked up the history of the game — I like to be prepared and informed — and learned that bid whist originated in London somewhere around the 1700s and has now become a staple in the Black community regardless of social class. Lawyers and even the guy who you see riding a bike down grandma's street knows how to play and will talk shit to back it up. Count your President Barack Obama as a player (*I'd guess a very good one*) and while I can't confirm it, U.S. Congresswoman Sheila Jackson Lee plays with her shoes off and talks a lot of noise. She talks throughout the game and probably has a special set of cards just in case someone feels like playing.

And that's just it. Real card players know that before you start a game, you have to know the rules. You need to know a person's rules before you sit down at the table.

In spades, I play with the jokers, the first hand bids itself and we don't carry the sandbags. If we are playing at my house, we are using my cards and I'm dealing first. You can go blind if you are down by 100, and I want those three books if you renege. I expect you are paying attention to the game because we aren't opening the books to check the cards that were played. And get your cards off the table. If not, I will pick them up and keep them for myself, and use the points to beat you. My house. My rules.

Everyone plays the game differently, so it's best

that you understand what you are dealing with before you get started. It allows for limited confusion, minimum arguments, and for friendships to remain intact.

Here's the thing. These card games are the only time I follow rules. I've been known to show up to events out of uniform, skip a stop sign if the coast is clear and it is late at night. I rarely wear matching socks and have the audacity to believe that you can wear polka dots and stripes together. When you look around my house, you won't find a set of anything. My plan has gotten me this far in life. Why should I stop now?

I've picked up the perfect interview question to use when I am looking to fill a vacancy — are you a rule breaker or a rule follower? Every time I've asked it, the candidate has paused and pondered for an extended period of time. They all have the same look on their face. I've guessed that most are trying to determine if there's a specific answer that I'm looking for or if they want to actually tell me the truth. For the record, there's no right answer. I've hired both rule breakers and rule followers. It comes down to what I need at the moment.

There is value in a person who follows the rules. They keep you out of trouble. They usually know the details of what is happening, the day's itinerary, and they know what is due and when. They are highly focused and understand the need and the ramifications of order. On the other hand, rule breakers are spontaneous. Often, they need to be reminded of the start time and are always ready for whatever. On a good team — you need both. You need balance and coverage.

It wasn't until later in life that I realized I was not a rule follower. I've never seen it that way. I understand that rules matter. I just have not seen how they apply to me. Over time, I've learned that rules are usually created to force people into a habit or pattern. Rules are designed to protect the masses. Think about it — we've been told our whole life to follow a pattern. The nursery rhyme "first comes love, then comes marriage, then comes a baby in a baby carriage" tells us how our life was supposed to happen. We were taught to color in the lines. We eat dessert last. There are countless people who were told to make their bed every day to lead to a day of less stress. I read something while I was pregnant that said I shouldn't cut my hair and I've read that men shouldn't wear pink.

There are hundreds of books written about how these standard habits create a lifestyle that is predictable and safe. A life that is easy for others to digest. On that same aisle in the bookstore, there's another set of books. These books challenge the status quo — these writers encourage us to color outside the lines, try something different and live outside the box. Malcolm Gladwell's popular book, "Outliers," challenges the whole notion of hard work leading to success. Instead, he talks about context and timing.

See there's no tried-and-true formula that can be followed to achieve success. There's no box. What I know to be true is that the rules we are told to follow are good guardrails for life. They are designed to help us understand what's right and appropriate. I've also seen that these guardrails create an opportunity for innovation and creation. I often challenge the status quo and think we should re-examine why we created the original rule in the first place.

I used to dream about making it to the C-Suite. I worked my entire career following someone's rules (*go figure that*) to ensure I had chief in my title. Once I made it and was being onboarded, I was told I needed to swipe in to the time clock every day. Pause. I was supposed to be there by 8:00 a.m. (*late is 8:06*) and I had to walk over to a time clock and swipe my badge to report that I was at work. In all my dreams of how my life would be once I made it to the C-Suite, I never saw myself in a sharp blazer, swiping a time clock. In fact, in all my favorite movies — "Boomerang" and "Devil Loves Prada" — the bad bitch in charge never once had a badge and worried about being on time. She usually had an assistant who was waiting for her with her standard coffee drink. In most of the scenes, work was done somewhere else — not in an office. There was never a conversation about the time clock. And come to think of it, nobody had a badge.

In my real life at my job where I had landed in the C-Suite, these folks were serious about the time clock. I wasn't interested in ruining my own dreams, so I never clocked in.

My colleague came to visit my office one afternoon and gave me a very serious speech about the importance of clocking in and how it balanced out the system, removed inequities, protected the organization, etc. She was serious in her reprimand and used her professional voice while never cracking a smile.

Never once did she make it clear how the rule impacted me and my situation. She didn't talk about what I should do if I have a meeting offsite prior to the start of the day. She went into detail of how the rule of clocking in was designed years back to stop employees from "stealing time" and as such, everyone — no matter their role or title — was required to clock in every single day.

I wasn't convinced. To me, it seemed like the rule was arbitrarily made or that the rule was made to be broken. How were employees being paid for work being done away from their work site? What happened when employees genuinely forgot to clock in? What about the Saturdays I worked at community events? Where was my coffee? Nothing about it made sense to me.

I'm imagining you reading this and wondering how or why my brain worked this way? Why was I challenging a simple rule? I should just clock in. I passed it on my way to my office, and it was really not a big deal. I know. It's strange. But, as the popular meme says, "Sis, the rules are fake. Do you." I didn't clock in for weeks. Nothing happened. I never missed a paycheck, and no one said anything.

The clock-in procedure was put in place by someone to make their life easier. The process was designed to make time and attendance make sense to them and as the organization changed and as practices evolved, the same rule remained, but the rationale didn't quite make sense anymore. There were people who worked varying schedules and at varying locations. The fact that work was only done in an organization's facility was also a contradiction.

To this day, I don't know how my time is tracked or if there's someone who is cursing every week to make sure I get a check. I don't care.

There are plenty of "clocking in" rules that many of us are following and reciting over and over again. If you start simple, you'll wonder why you don't eat pancakes in the afternoon or why you still think you can't wear white after Labor Day. A little more complicated and even taboo — you don't drink in front of your parents, you must wear matching socks and wouldn't imagine opening your birthday gifts before your actual birthday.

These orthodoxies shape the way we live. They aren't rules — just simply habits, guiding principles or beliefs that we've developed throughout our life. Many of them are passed down through our families or culture and are designed to keep life in order, us consistent and to make things simply make sense. Friends, the rules aren't real. Well, there are real rules — the ones designed to keep us safe, the ones that are expedient (*get us to heaven*) and the ones that keep us employed, married and out of jail.

These are not the rules I'm talking about. I'm talking about the rules that we've made up. The ones that force us to compete against ourselves, impose crazy deadlines on us or our friends, and force us to live in frustration and defeat.

Friends, the rules aren't real.

I have a friend whose son has autism. When I tell you this mama is serious. She keeps his life in order, knows what he needs, advocates for him and knows the ins and outs of autism. I won't be surprised if she quits her job and launches an organization designed to focus on changing the outcomes of young men like her son. In talking, she briefly mentioned how she wished she understood how he was feeling since he couldn't articulate with words.

It was at that moment I reminded her of just how fake the rules are. I told her that we don't need words to communicate. Never once in his life has she wondered if he enjoyed what she cooked. She could always tell how he feels about people as soon as he meets them. She knew when he wasn't feeling well and he made it clear when he was ready to play, watch TV or go to bed. Her son has found other ways to communicate. Her looking for him to talk and being frustrated that he couldn't was following the rules. The fake rules.

These made up rules are based on an array of ideas, dreams and the fairy tales that we've read, dreamt up or saw play out in the movies. We are following people on Instagram and have decided their lifestyle is one we should have as well. Those rules.

There's nothing that says you have to stay at your job. You absolutely can quit your job without having something else lined up. There's no reason you can't become a lawyer after 30 and surely you can have a baby after 40. Hi, I'm here as proof.

There are a ton of examples out there where the rule just makes little sense. COVID-19 made it so. No longer do we have to gather and celebrate babies and brides with a standard shower. Those new drive-by parties are the saving grace. You no longer have to sit through opening gifts and those clothespin games are a thing of the past. Just drive up, smile and drop your gift off and the guest of honor is officially "showered."

I'm here to tell you that there is not a single reason many of us should be going to an office building (*let alone clocking in*) to do our work. C-19 proved that we can be efficient and productive in our pajamas. And, if you ask the banks — those buildings are expendable. People are doing their financial transactions online. So now, what rules, again?

I have a perfect example of what rules? Auntie Tab. You know her as Tabitha Brown. This lady went bananas — she has a clothing line with Target, is doing voice-overs, launched a TV show, a line of cooking seasoning, wrote a book and went on tour based on a few posts on the internet via her phone! She didn't audition for the part. And while she lives in LA, she didn't have to be there to "make it."

There simply are no rules. You create the rules and change them when you want.

Once you get to the place where you can accept that the rules weren't designed to make you famous or help you get to financial freedom, you'll be in a better mind space. You'll understand that you sometimes have to follow the directions. You'll decide when to push the envelope or ask for forgiveness after you've done something, rather than asking for approval upfront.

We have a "rule" in my house. Basically, if there's a major purchase, we should talk to the other person in advance. Not for approval, but as an opportunity for feedback — to confirm we aren't making a crazy decision in haste or by chance we aren't spending a lot of money at the same time. Well, my husband broke the rule. He purchased some property without giving me the opportunity to weigh in. At the end of the day, I couldn't be mad. If he would have followed the rule, I probably would have said no, asked a few too many questions, then some more questions and before you know it, he would have missed a deal of a lifetime. The rules are fake. You don't have to follow them. I would warn you, though, that you have to live with the consequences, whatever they are.

The Bottom Line.

The self-imposed rules are fake. You can break them, you can follow them — do what you want. Look at the rules as an opportunity to try something outside of our comfort zone. Oftentimes, rules do not serve us and are based on mistaken beliefs. These self-imposed rules are critical and judgmental. They can make us feel overwhelmed and stuck by making things more complicated or rigid than they need to be.

A Little More.

I don't walk around the world thinking that I am exempt from anything. Rather, I walk through life with the promise that I am taking accountability for my own decisions and actions rather than being led by external influences and requirements. I'd encourage you too to challenge the status quo to learn the rules, so you can break them.

Your Turn.

- Consider how you have used the rules to stop you from winning in the game of life?

- Are you using the rules to keep you stagnated and as an excuse to stay inside the box?

_____

_____

_____

_____

_____

_____

_____

_____

_____

_____

_____

_____

_____

_____

_____

_____

_____

_____

_____

Like Who Likes You.

One fact about me: I've got a story for everything. But my favorite stories usually include my husband. The first one that involves him is the very birth of our relationship. We were introduced by a stranger. I've also been harassed by two teenage girls and their older brother while vacationing on Manhattan Beach in Los Angeles, California because of him.

Yes, it's just like that. There's never been a vacation where we have been able to go and people not treat him like he's a celebrity. Usually it's because they think he's Rick Ross. I know what you are thinking — yeah right. But it is true. The people absolutely think he is Rick Ross, the millionaire rapper who owns hundreds of Wingstop restaurants, drinks champagne out of the bottle and drives expensive fancy cars. My husband is not a big fan of Wingstop, is not a heavy drinker, and doesn't spend his money on automobiles.

What I have concluded is that he's a larger dude, wears designer shades, has a beard and may have a few extra dollars in his pocket that allows him to vacation at all-inclusive luxury resorts. It doesn't stop there. Somehow my husband becomes the OG, the Unk, or Big Cuz to whomever he meets. He's reasonable, a good listener and asks difficult questions, challenges thinking and once he adds in his one-liners, people are hooked.

While he's pretty amazing and I count my blessings every night, he's not at all the person I thought I'd marry. As a teenage girl, I was totally attracted to the bad boys. The dudes who had the freshest kicks, flashiest rims, and the quick-witted tongues. The more tattoos and violent tendencies, the better. These guys were also the dudes who made you wait by the phone and caused you to wonder if you were the only woman he was entertaining.

I've heard that every girl marries her father or a fantasized version of him. I never thought this would happen for me and couldn't see the logic. Most likely because my dad wasn't someone I got along with when I was a teenager. I wanted the exact opposite of him.

After my parents divorced, I wasn't excited about seeing my dad. And if I'm being honest, I think the feeling was mutual. We were trying to learn to operate under new terms all while experiencing our own stages of grief from the divorce. There were a lot of fireworks and mis-understandings that led to a few exchanges that should never have happened between a daughter and her father. You can ask my brother about the potential rat poisoning episode, and my mom can tell you about the few months where I ignored my dad and how she had to cautiously navigate that, including signing me up for coun-seling. It wasn't an easy time for any of us.

After a few years of a rocky relationship, we got it together. Seeing us together now, you'd never guess I wasn't always daddy's little girl. He's my hero and I am quick to call him to swoop in and save the day.

I remember the day our relationship changed for the better. I was 17 years old.

It started with a simple question. I cautiously asked him what I had done to him to make him be so short, cold and mean, particularly to me. He was constantly irritable, talked with an elevated tone and I was over it. We were driving through Houston's medical center. An area that is not easy to navigate between lights, crosswalks, ambulances and pedestrians. I asked him the question straight and without any fanfare. I didn't wait for a red light. I just blurted it out. This is how I am even now, confronting things head on. Now that I look back, this is how I've always been.

My dad responded with silence. Once he started talking, I didn't think it would end. He started at his beginning and filled me in on his upbringing. He talked about the fact that he didn't have support from his dad. He reminded me that his dad, the grandfather I had met only once, was not always around while he was growing up and that I was lucky to even have a father that was in my life.

Before I knew it, I spouted off my rebuttal. Simply put, I said to him that I didn't ask to be born. I reminded him that he and my mom made a decision to get married and live the American dream with two children. I spoke on the decision that they made to fight a statistic that falsely painted a picture that Black families were made up of single-parent homes and continued my counterargument to remind him that despite being a little annoying, I, his daughter, didn't embarrass him. I stayed out of trouble, made decent grades, and frankly, was the daughter that many of his friends wished they had.

My memory of that conversation doesn't include tears, hugs or high fives. I don't know if he apologized or if we kept talking about current events, the news or something else. What I do remember is that the conversation set me free. Free to be open enough to find and date a man that was full of flaws, yet open enough to meet me where I am and love me no matter what. My attraction to bad boys didn't change, but I got the big picture.

In that moment, Dad was vulnerable but open enough to see how his daughter was being impacted by choices he was making in his life and he adjusted. I hope he respects that I could have a conversation with him and that I was begging for a different relationship. I grew closer to my father and realized that he was a great example of a man.

I can't fast forward to the end of the story just yet. I need to share that for almost 15 years after that conversation, I was single and mingling. I was meeting people, building friendships, making connections and living life. In that time period, I had some friends, a few situationships, went on a lot of dates and had some periods of solitude. During each phase, I learned what I liked and what I didn't like.

Graduate school was a special time for me. You'd think balancing a full-time job, full-time graduate-level course work, and at-home reading and studying would have me stressed out. Not at all. Your girl was outside and in these streets. Every Thursday night after class, the class crew made up of young working adults would load up and carpool to the most popular nightclub of the week. There are a lot of stories that I'll share one day with my sons (*they won't believe any*) but there are few things that are connected to finding the real one that can be shared here.

One outing, I rolled out of bed straight to the club. No preparation, no special outfit or make-up. The night was crazy. Lots of drinking, dancing and laughing. Out of the corner of my eye, I saw a guy in the corner. He watched me the entire night. I saw him and continued my single girl antics. He sent a round of drinks over to our section to get my attention. That was enough to send him my number.

We spent the next few days in a whirlwind of talking and texting. It was right up my alley — a whirlwind of courtship. Flowers, dinners, outings and VIP seats wherever we went. He said he was a college football coach and had finished the season early and as a result he was staying with his parents at a house he owned. He explained to me how he let them stay in the house while he was out of town working.

While I am a lot of things, observant is one of my favorite descriptors. Once I visited, I noticed a curio cabinet filled with antique birds and a coffee maker on the kitchen counter. I had a few thoughts: What 20-something single man drinks coffee? A curio cabinet set off an alarm, but the decorated towels are really what took me out. They weren't just folded and hung on the bar in the bathroom. These towels had lace on them and were folded in such a pretty and warm way. I was clear that this home did not belong to a single man. The fact that he was living at home with his parents wasn't the turn off. I only told you a piece of the story. We had a good time but, good Lord, he was a liar. Everything was a lie.

Then, there was my ex who didn't talk. Two years of silence. He bought awesome gifts, and we took amazing vacations, but the dude didn't say a word most days. It didn't work out.

I spent a few weeks hanging out with a tall, dark and handsome guy. This guy was perfect on paper. He was well paid, funny and very kind. But when he drank, he drank. I never knew what would happen and was always on my toes. After a few drinks at dinner, he was usually slumped over and drooling. Every single time he went out with his friends, I got a call to come and get him. I knew that this wasn't about to be my life and it served as the perfect sign for me to move on.

Once I met a guy on an airplane. I felt sick and he held the throw up bag while I vomited my guts out. He spent the entire flight patting my back and comforting me. I think it was love at first sight. Who wouldn't want a man who is nurturing and has a strong stomach? These were my thoughts between coughs. I was sure that our love story would be one that people would find unbelievable and quite enchanting. It was going to be perfect. Once our flight landed, those dreams fizzled quickly. Our work schedules couldn't align. Apparently, he flew a lot.

During a work sales trip, I exchanged numbers

with a potential client. It took a few weeks for us to actually connect in person. We talked on the phone a lot about music and Houston culture. I later found out he had two kids and another on the way. That was where I left the stage.

I won't share details about the college friend who made his way back in my life, but wanted me to change my work schedule to be with him or the guy who had a problem with me going to church every Sunday.

So you can imagine that when I decided to give dating a break, I did it with good cause. I absolutely needed a break. I needed time to rest my nerves. Time to be alone. Time to detox from the foolishness of the dating pool that was filled with pee.

And I did just that. As the end of the year approached, I decided I would be single and use the new year to focus on my new job and me. For the next few months, I was laser focused on myself and ensuring I succeeded at work. Shortly into the year, I was sent to a conference in Charlotte. This was the perfect time for me to rest, eat room service food and unwind from several weeks of a very long commute to and from work.

The conference was uneventful. I learned a few things and did a little networking. I had purposely chosen a seat next to a guy who looked boring. I figured he would be focused on the learnings and would have all the notes. He had the notes, but he also talked my ear off. He asked me thousands of questions. He wanted to know my five-year and 10-year career plans. He was quick to share all his goals — from financial to the timing of his next child and where he wanted to work while pursuing his ultimate career move. Like a nice professional, I smiled. I laughed. But I really just wanted to get under the covers in my bed and watch TV in my pajamas. I cared nothing about his plans and surely wasn't thinking about what or where I would be in the next five years. On the third day of our conference, we skipped the reception and went to dinner. I don't know why I did it, but it paid off.

Over dinner he asked more questions (*this guy!!*). More about my family, my hopes, my dreams and even about my friends. As we were at the end of our meal, he asked if I had a boyfriend. My response was easy — no and I wasn't looking either. I was annoyed by him. I had put my guard down and somehow I was giving off a vibe that I was interested. He wasn't my type at all and to make matters worse, he was wearing a wedding ring. I think he picked up on my response of disgust and quickly rolled his eyes and went on to talk about a friend who had just moved to my city.

Nothing about his overview of his friend excited me. But I agreed to talk to him one time. He called him right there on the spot and handed me the phone.

A deep southern drawl said, "What's up?" I swear he spoke in slow motion. My eyebrow raised. I could tell he was polite and full of confidence. We exchanged pleasantries and he asked if he could call me later. I obliged. Before I made it to my room, he had already called me. My other eyebrow went up. I wasn't positive if I was intrigued most by his clear show of interest and follow through or concerned that I'd picked up a stalker.

We talked and texted nonstop over the next few days. I learned a lot about him. He shared his background and how he ended up in Houston. We talked about his goals, favorite songs and how he spent his teen years pretending he was an adult. He told me how much he loved New Jack Swing and thought he was moving to Philadelphia and wanted to marry Jill Scott. He said he was a scholar and not an athlete and I listened to him talk about fraternity life and his extended collegiate experience. I told him my college story and talked about my family. I talked about my love of naps and how I was not a morning person. He laughed at my stories about my dad and asked a lot of questions about my mom. He wanted to know about my job and listened when I talked about the TV show I was watching. It was easy to have a light conversation with him. We both agreed we weren't looking for a relationship but liked the conversation. I did ask him if he was interested in a relationship or tour guide of the city? His tour guide response led me to let my guard down. I had not seen him and wasn't planning on making time once I made it home after the conference.

Only issue, our conversations never stopped. If we weren't talking, we were texting. There wasn't a rush to what we were doing, which means we never saw each other or sent pictures. Once we exchanged "MySpace" handles, I realized that he met not a single piece of my criteria. None. He was nice looking but at the time, I was looking for Chris Weber (*tall basketball player from 1991-93 Michigan University basketball team with a lot of swag*). I am not sure how he felt about me, but I will tell you the calls increased. He called more and made an effort to let me know he was interested. And just like that the tour guide concept went out the door and things got a little complicated.

Once we were both settled in Houston, he turned up the heat and invited me to dinner, pushed to have day dates and connect whenever I had free time. After some back and forth, we agreed to meet following a girls' night that was planned for months. That girls' night ended after midnight. I was hoping it was too late to connect, so I didn't call. Like clockwork, though, he called to check if I had made it home safely and invited me out. I could hear my mom remind me of what was open at midnight. She forgot that Denny's was open 24 hours a day. That's where we met.

As I pulled up, he jumped out of the car with a huge smile. It was clear he was happy to see me. He held my door and escorted me inside. We sat down and our waitress came over. She introduced herself as Charlotte. We immediately laughed as it was ironic because, technically, we met in Charlotte. That's where I was when we were introduced.

Our dating journey went pretty fast. He made it clear that whoever else I was seeing was going to have to work to see me. If I remember correctly, I took a nap on his couch after our official first date. It was a required after church nap before I went to the grocery store. I did this every single week and didn't plan to stop. While I slept, he didn't bother me at all. In fact, my ex-boyfriend called while I was there. I looked at his number and rolled over and drifted off. That moment sealed the deal. I knew I had met the one.

I didn't show it. I made him work hard. He called every day as I left work. He constantly asked me if I ate, what I needed and he was genuinely concerned about my day. He sent flowers and called the office to check on me. He asked if he could kiss me and wanted to know about my parents' well-being. He held my hand and called me gorgeous.

The boy had game, but I was playing right along with him. I didn't answer all the time and once or twice, I went to dinner with someone else. I needed him to stay on his toes.

I say it all the time to anyone who is dating... like who likes you. I didn't exactly take my advice. I was running from a relationship with someone who had made it crystal clear that he wanted me. I didn't do this because I didn't like him. I did like him, but I had created a list of things my husband should do based on past experiences. I wanted him to be older, an entrepreneur, tall, from Houston. He was not any of those. Over the weeks of our courting, we had grown close. I enjoyed his company. We were spiritually aligned, our values were similar, we had a lot in common, had similar goals and he was kinda cute. I was just looking for "something" else.

I called my mom and told her my dilemma. She laughed. A loud, hearty laugh. It was long and went from a giggle to a cackle. Once she gathered herself, she said, "I don't understand the problem."

I went through the situation again. "There's this guy who likes me—a lot. He's good company and he's funny."

"And?" she said, waiting for more. Her words hit hard in only the way a mama can deliver a gut punch. It was full of judgment and finality. I didn't have a rebuttal. She ended our conversation by saying, "like who likes you."

I'll fast forward a little more. I married the dude who was kinda cute and called me before dinner was over. I've been his tour guide ever since. We have a great life. Our time together has not been without challenge, but I can't imagine navigating the hard stuff with anyone else. He puts up with my silent treatments in the morning and knows just the right amount of space I need to do me. He pushed me out my comfort zone and is one of the few people who can make me chill when I'm in one of my moods. He cheers loud for me and gets that I will forever have a full calendar and a whole bunch of irons in the fire. He laughs at everything and can hustle (*or nicely ask*) for anything. We've been to museums, the hole-in-the-wall club and dressed up for galas. He beats me to church and buys me food. I am sure he was pretty much made for me.

I've caught myself sharing my mom's advice (*probably with the same tone*) to so many others. Many times it's about relationships, but the sentiment can be applied to more than just that.

I've given this advice to my friends as they were dating, to college students as they selected a major, and even reminded myself while weighing options for job offers. In those conversations, I've come to learn that many of us have chosen to pursue the hard stuff rather than lean into embracing something that is comfortable and easy because we have an idea of what something should be. That is often based on the false notion that there's something wrong with things being easy and carefree.

This is the same concept many of us choose as we navigate life and love. We often choose the most difficult route and find comfort in trying to conquer it. We're taught to pick something and stick with it. Some of us may have even heard that if you want something, you have to work for it. And the work implies that you have to give it your all, chase it, pursue it, and fight through the discomfort.

But what if we picked the easier option? The option that was easy and made us feel comfortable? The option that "liked us." I am not lactose intolerant (*Thank God! I love cheese.*) but I know plenty of people who are. They know the consequences of eating cheese or ice cream. It's quite simple — their body doesn't like it and rejects it. Yet, without fail, they will get the largest milkshake and smile while eating it and end up complaining about a stomachache.

I can't imagine what would have happened if I would have passed on the opportunity to meet the guy my friend had in mind for me. At the time, without even knowing I was lactose intolerant and looking for a milkshake! When what I needed was standing right in front of me, pursuing and choosing me. It wasn't until I paused and realized I was running away from something that I had asked for and maybe even prayed for in hopes that one day I just may get it. Mom's comment helped me to realize that what I needed was right in front of me...my answered prayer.

The Bottom Line.

There's an urban mantra— go where you are celebrated, not tolerated. The phrase is meant to encourage you to choose places, people, and things where the red carpet is rolled out in honor of you. You are celebrated and appreciated and valued. This concept is very much aligned with my thoughts around the concept of liking who likes you. While I used it to describe a romantic relationship, the concept can be applied to any "relationship" in your life, whether it's a work environment, friendship or organizations. I dare you to connect with people and things that are attracted to you. Things that add value to you, people that pour into you and celebrate you when you aren't there. Stay close to people that get you and choose you.

A Little More.

When someone or something likes you, you will know. It will be clear and there won't be any question around the matter. If there are questions and wonderings then the answer is no. It doesn't like you and you should move on.

Your Turn.

• Can you imagine if you only went places where you were celebrated?

• What would happen if you only accepted what brought you joy and overwhelmed your heart with love?

- What "likes" you? How do you know?

- Are there things that clearly do not like you? What are you doing to separate yourself from them?

_____

_____

_____

_____

_____

_____

_____

_____

_____

_____

_____

_____

_____

_____

_____

_____

_____

_____

_____

_____

_____

_____

_____

_____

_____

_____

_____

_____

_____

_____

_____

_____

_____

_____

_____

_____

_____

_____

_____

_____

For Such A
Time As This.

You were prepared for such times as this.

Technically, I've been doing communications and marketing work since second grade. That year, I won a speech contest. I beat out a super smart kindergartner and a fifth-grade boy with my awesome essay about being a proud Houstonian. My prize was a photo opportunity with the mayor of the city and my school's principal.

I can't recite or even recall the essay today. I wouldn't even be able to tell you anything more than what I wore that day — a white lace dress, tights and a white bow to match. I only know that because there's a photo from the event in my family's archives.

I can vividly remember skipping afternoon playtime at my grandmother's house for an entire week to come up with just the right statements that would make my classmates laugh and my teachers smile. I wanted to win and I knew I was going to. I just needed to get the words in the right order.

There's also a picture of me collecting my trophy. I'm not giddy or smiling hard. It's like I was there for business. When I look at that picture, I am tickled. It is a reminder to me that even before I knew what I'd be doing as an adult (*or what I was going to be when I grew up*) I was being prepared to do it.

Each leg of my career journey has prepared me for the next segment. I've been able to build on the things I've done and people I've met and use them to be successful. Those relationships have worked together to create some amazing things. One I am so proud of is the Impact Leadership Academy in Aldine ISD. The all-boys school was created in conjunction with Prairie View A&M University. I also love the magazine we birthed at Prairie View. *1876*, was a labor of love that pushed me past anything I've ever done. I partnered with a lot of people to get each issue designed and in the hands of alumni and supporters. I could only do that because of my experience with writing and editing.

I am not a Bible scholar by any stretch of the imagination but I know that the idea — you were prepared for such a time as this — speaks to Ester, a woman of the Bible, who is positioned to make a choice. There is a lot counting on her decision. The conditions and history of her life aren't in her favor. No one told her in advance that she'd be put in a place that may impact future generations. I encourage you to read the entire book of Ester to understand all of the intricacies of Ester and how they all work together. The really good part starts in Chapter 4 but the key message is Ester 4:14. Additionally, with one Google search of her name and her story, you'll see a host of commentary about her influence.

The phrase, You are Prepared for Such a Time as This, is spoken to her and thought to provide a reminder that, perhaps, everything happens the way it happens for a reason. She's given the reminder that her courage is based on the notion that someone — God — is bigger than her and is orchestrating a future that she can't see or even imagine.

I've had many FSATAT (*For Such A Time As This*) moments throughout my life, especially in my career. But one phone call to a colleague made it clear to me that like Ester, I have been consistently positioned to impact those around me. And I have everything I need already in me.

The phone call happened while I was managing a major crisis, balancing an unsupportive supervisor, and interacting with colleagues who were underprepared for their roles and in over their heads. As the voice of the organization, I was expected to make sense of the problem and be prepared to share and support our solution to a variety of stakeholders in a short period of time. Sometimes that was easy. I simply translated what I heard into language that made sense to the average person. Other times, I asked hard questions, pushed back on our responses and questioned if we were really doing what our processes and procedures called for before even getting to the place where I could say it to the public. This was one of those times where nothing we were saying made sense to me. I was tired of asking questions and people were sick of seeing my number show up on their caller ID.

I had reached a plateau and didn't have the answer. I was done, burned out, and ready to throw in the towel. I called my colleague, who was in another state, for a brain break. While she had no clue about the issue I was dealing with, I knew she would understand because she worked in a similar role. She answered the phone and I went in.

I am sure I was speaking random gibberish. I know I wasn't making sense as I was pouring out my heart, explaining the problem, becoming frustrated and asking for help. I explained the best way I could that I didn't know what to do and was probably going to quit and let someone else deal with it. I started recanting the mistakes I had made in my life. I was telling her about things I had done in college and recalling feedback I had received during evaluations and by my supervisors. Frankly, I was in a bad place. My confidence was leaking out and I was beginning to doubt how I even got the job in the first place. As I learned in a leadership course, I was in the basement. I wasn't able to see my way out of the problem and was focused on the negatives. Being in the basement caused me not to see any light or hope.

Once I finally took a break from talking, she reminded me of all the "hard things" I had already done. She reminded me that what I was dealing with was similar to challenges I had handled in the past. And the last piece of advice she gave me was that what I had done in my past — from the places I had visited, to the meetings I had attended, books I had read, issues I had — prepared me for this moment.

I gathered myself, took a walk around the building and did the work. I don't even remember what the work was, but I did it. I am positive that my colleagues didn't sense my frustration and by the next day, I had jumped three or four similar hurdles.

I am forever grateful for that moment and often reflect on our conversation. She was so right. I've had moments since then when I've wondered how I ended up in a crazy conundrum or what rabbit I was going to pull out my hat.

I have a mentor who has let me in on the thought process behind some of her hiring decisions. Without fail, during every search she falls in love with a candidate who is full of energy and charisma. In her eyes, the candidate has such promise and seems eager to do a good job. The candidate interviews well and she can sense how the person will bring energy and light to her team.

But when compared to the experienced candidate who's worked their way up the ladder, there usually is no decision to be made. The candidate with potential is just that: someone who has potential and is eager to bring ideas to the table.

On the other hand, the tenured candidate brings more to the team than just experience. This person brings grit from problem solving and learning how a role fits in the bigger picture of an organization. This candidate brings experiences with difficult colleagues and knows how to find ways to successfully complete a job with limited resources and support.

Her pragmatic approach has stuck with me: people can't be fast tracked into leadership. The best leaders have been followers. They have experiences that don't always show up on a resumé but always show up in the workplace. You don't go from being a freshman on the B team one year to competing for an Olympic gold medal in the next summer games. That's a silly thought. As you climb the competition ladder, you take what you learn and apply it to the next opportunity—building a bank of skills that have prepared you more than you could have ever imagined.

I've almost done every role in the area of communications. As an intern, I stuffed and licked envelopes. I faxed and answered the phone. I got coffee and ordered lunch. I can't count the number of paper cuts I collected along the way or the times I dropped coffee or messed up the lunch order.

Finally, I figured out a system and created a tool to wet the back of the envelope before the office purchased self-sticking ones. I also started pre-ordering coffee and stocked the office with all kinds of drinks. I've done seating charts, stayed late and come in early.

So when I ask somebody to do something, it's not because I don't want to do it. It is because I've already done it and believe that I could be limiting others by not giving them the opportunity to experience growth and the opportunity to learn. I think that that's the concept of you being prepared For Such A Time As This because if you skip these steps or days when you have to lick envelopes and label them correctly on your way to becoming an executive, you may not value that somebody literally had to stuff the envelopes that are being sent on your behalf.

My brother learned how to build a website in about 18 hours. He locked himself in a room and just dug in and learned it. Since then, he's been called on by companies across the world for his expertise in the software. He's taught others and has secured contracts because of his ability to use the software to its full capacity. I asked him why he did it that way and he said it's a chip on his shoulder; he's trying to prove a point to himself. He didn't do it because someone told him to or challenged him. It was his own doing. I don't know if the chip runs in the family or what, but I've got the same problem. There's some things I do just because I can or because I want to know how or the steps it takes to do them. It's a strong possibility that it's in our genetics. Mom is the same way and my dad leads the pack.

I will work harder than most people, go above and beyond, and do whatever it takes for a project to be completed. I've pulled 24-hour shifts and brought breakfast to the early morning meeting.

There's also this: I'm consistently one of very few Black women or Black people in the room. As hard as it is to admit it, I've learned that that's the way it goes. You work hard and do what you have to do and are asked to speak for anyone who looks like you.

I've sat in rooms where people expressed their opinion on how to message something to Black parents. I was the only person of color and the only communicator. I've rewritten statements about fights on campus — removing the word brawl — and pitched a story to the media about a star student-athlete who had great catches, test scores AND happened to be Black. I left the race part out on purpose when I talked to the media outlet.

I bring up color simply because it's still a factor today. It is still what leads the conversation. I'm aware that people see me as a Black woman and even more aware that everyone believes they can do communications. Although I've had great work experience, an undergraduate and master's degree in communications, I pursued an accreditation to help separate me from the pack, to separate me from being a practitioner to being someone who could lead strategic conversations and execute comprehensive plans rather than just cross items off a to-do list. I have always been a strong team player and always did my best. I knew that having those letters behind my name brought more to the table.

It wasn't an easy journey. I squeezed in studying wherever I could and carried flash cards in my purse. When I stood on stage and was pinned in 2018, I realized I was the only Black APR in school communications in Texas. I wasn't surprised, but I recognized even more why it was important to have the credentials.

I could go through my resumé of jobs but that's boring. The truth is while each role has been a different assignment, with different communities and objectives, the goal has remained the same: tell the organizational story. The story of the people.

I never would've thought that what I do now would be at all related to what I would've been doing. When I was younger, I swore that I was going to be a sports agent. Then, I switched to being a sports broadcaster. I wanted to be on the sidelines reporting the action. I actually spent some time working at a local radio station as an intern. It was an amazing experience and I'm forever indebted to Houston sports broadcaster and Texas Radio Hall of Famer, Ralph Cooper. He's a legend in the sports world who turned over some valuable air time to a novice who wanted to talk about current events and the culture of sports.

I also wanted to be a therapist, psychotherapist or psychologist, and I can't tell you why exactly other than I was so intrigued by how people's minds work. Truth is, I've utilized my interest in all those areas in some role in one way or another.

I jumped into school communications in the way I have approached so many other areas in my life — head first. This time it was for Texas' largest school district. On the day of my interview, news dropped that a top official was arrested for possession of a controlled substance. My start was delayed because an ice storm hit the area and shut down fingerprinting for days. And if that wasn't enough warning, on my first day I learned that campuses in minority neighborhoods would be closing.

Little did I know that I would be able to draw from all my experiences — from being born and raised in Houston, to having parents who graduated from local schools, to knowing principals, teachers, parents and leaders in the district. I never would have imagined that the media interviews I did at my previous job would prepare me to stand in front of a camera and talk with clarity and understanding.

Because I was a reporter, I could connect with reporters assigned to the district in new and different ways. There's a funny story about a reporter I met because he said my name incorrectly (*see the chapter called — It's Complicated*); this reporter has evolved into being one of my thought partners. Now, he says my full name correctly every time he addresses me.

Truly, I had been prepared for this time and so many others that are before me.

The Bottom Line.

Everything happens for a reason. Use the experience to prepare you for the next opportunity.

A Little More.

So far, you've survived 100% of your bad days. Based on our track record, you will make it through this one too.

Your Turn.

- Have you had a For Such A Time As This moment?
- What were the reminders that you had the tools and experiences to thrive?

_____

_____

_____

_____

_____

_____

_____

_____

_____

_____

_____

_____

_____

_____

_____

_____

_____

_____

_____

_____

_____

_____

_____

_____

_____

_____

_____

_____

_____

_____

_____

_____

_____

_____

_____

_____

_____

_____

_____

_____

_____

_____

_____

_____

_____

_____

_____

_____

_____

_____

_____

_____

_____

_____

_____

_____

_____

_____

_____

Stay Ready So
You Don't Have
to Get Ready.

I'm convinced that reading unlocks doors and challenges you to think beyond what you know. By reading, I've been exposed to entrepreneurship — through the "Babysitters Club" series and the "Family Business" series by Carl Weber. I've learned about the great migration by reading how millions of Blacks left places like Alabama, Mississippi and Georgia in hopes of identifying safety, resources and a better life in "Warmth of Other Suns" by Isabel Wilkerson. It continues to be my favorite book as it reminds me that not only is life complicated but you've got to do what you can with what you have. There's a million lessons in that book. I can't tell enough people to read it.

I learned about the art of self-care through "Eat, Pray, Love" and Elizabeth Gilbert's trope through Italy, India and Bali. I learned just how powerful our cells are as the Henrietta Lacks story gave us a deep dive into the complicated battle between science and life. It's an informative read but also a challenging one as I learned that her cells are the first human cells to be immortalized and they were around in the lab for 50 years before her family was aware. By the way, it's a great book that I would not have picked up if I had not heard about it from someone else.

We are a reading family, everybody from my parents to their grandkids. Before my oldest child was born, he had more books than most adults will have in their entire life. His library is diverse and includes the classics, Dr. Seuss and a children's Bible, and he even has a board book that lists out the various HBCUS, another one that illustrates the origin of rap, and another book that breaks down the various themes of standard architecture. Buddy is set. We have a few duplicates and have them stored and ready to be passed down to his younger brother.

His dad read to my belly every night from the time I announced I was pregnant until the baby came home. Dad packed a few books in his overnight bag and whipped them out to pass the time. The nurses got a kick out of it and joined in on the fun. Even now he pulls out a book and I can hear them reading it together. It is the sweetest sight.

For the first year, "Goodnight Moon" was in heavy rotation and now we've added a book about being a big brother and "100 First Words" to the list. I am trying to persuade him to read to his younger brother but most of the time they end up fighting over the book. I swear his first word was book and the pocket in front of his car seat has three to four spare books to help him stay focused on our commutes. Books are everywhere.

When I said we are a reading family, I meant it. While growing up, my brother and I would compete to read the most books and I have very clear memories of my mom carrying around a Danielle Steel paperback. I can see the newspaper sitting on the counter and, yes, we received the "Highlights" magazine every single month. For fun, we'd read through the encyclopedia set. We had the dark blue set of World Book Encyclopedias and the Encyclopedia Britannica. To this day, he and I exchange books and he has a mighty collection of books focused on Blacks and business, hip hop and sneakers. For birthdays or Christmas, you should expect a book or a gift card to a book store. That's just how it goes. Last year, I had a frank and candid conversation with my dad about the quality of his gifts over the years. It was my way of telling him not to torture another generation, his grandsons, with his specific type of gift giving.

Every year, we got exactly the same gift for every single occasion. He gave us a historical fiction book or an autobiography from Half Price Books (*Yes, it was used.*) and he hid a crisp bill inside. The bill might be a $100 or a $20, you just never knew. It was the luck of the draw and it depended on his mood.

The idea is that you'd have to read the book to find the money. When I tell people this story, they are so intrigued. They seem amazed at the thoughtfulness and reminder to read at a young age. He rewarded us for seeking knowledge. Years later, I have come to value the exposure to books and so many historical figures but as a kid it wasn't cool. It wasn't cool at all. My friends were sharing how they received new shoes, video games and clothes, while I could share that I got a book. A used book.

The funny part is that I always read the book. Every single time. I've read about Howard Hughes, the billionaire who was both a movie producer and airline owner. I still count "Makes Me Wanna Holler" by Nathan McCall as one of the best books I've ever read. Walter Mosley, my dad's favorite author, is one of the greatest authors of all time. I'd argue with anyone about it. While the covers weren't always the most inviting and the condition of the book was questionable, I was drawn to read and finish the book.

In the reader's world, there's a book trend called stacking. It's a great concept. A quick and easy way to see into people's minds. Essentially, you put together a stack of several books and show them off. I've seen them done for TBR (*to be read*) and others to highlight themes like the year's best chick lit or authors of color. I've seen a stack of favorite mysteries and stacks based on simply the color of the cover. I took the concept of stacking to heart and used it to create personalized stacks for my sons to pose with during their newborn photos.

The photo session stacks were created to be a reminder that knowledge is all around us and it was an ode to our family's love of reading. Each of their stacks was unique and filled with books that illustrated the culture, our history and a connection to the past. Jay Z's "Decoded," Barack Obama's "Audacity of Hope" and Malcolm X's memoir "By Any Means Necessary" were a few of the ones I selected. Each of the boys are sitting on top of the books. A reminder that knowledge is the foundation of all things.

And you guessed correctly, a few of those books were gifts from my father. His little trick worked. He was able to teach me something without lecturing and parent without doing much. Through his gift giving efforts, he taught me the importance of reading and how to use that knowledge to unlock doors.

That little key has turned into a major part of my life and I believe a reason I feel comfortable in so many spaces. It has helped me feel prepared and confident enough to walk into any space or place. I've found myself Googling information about organizations, groups and people as I met them. I read the reviews of restaurants before going and summaries of movies before buying the ticket. The more I know, the better I am prepared.

As my college graduation approached, I began searching for the right position to consider for my first job. During one round of interviews with a company I was very interested in joining, I was invited to dinner with the top executives. In my research, I came to understand that this type of interview was designed to determine if the candidate is able to communicate with others and can represent the organization in various settings. They aren't looking to measure your skill set. Instead, the hiring team is examining the soft, subtle skills that could determine if you are successful in the role.

While I have never truly suffered from stage fright or been nervous before speaking, interviewing or meeting new people, this time around I was nervous. The job opening was an ideal role at a very large advertising agency. The position was entry level, but I was promised an opportunity to move up quickly and train for other opportunities in the Houston office as preparation for placement in other offices across the country. I wanted this job and hoped to do well. There was a lot at stake. I didn't know what I would talk about or who would even be in attendance, but I was planning to walk away with a job.

I put on my best black dress, threw on my interview heels and prayed I'd do well. Long story short, I didn't get the job. Unfortunately 9/11 happened and the entire job field fell into shambles, causing many of us to find a new plan after college graduation that fall. What I will share is that I was a hit. As the Washington Mutual commercials says, I walked out of the interview, saying "Nailed It!" I was holding court as the old people say. I was chatting it up with everyone at the table about everything. We talked about the importance of drinking water to sports and even historical moments from the Olympics. We even discussed a few current events and touched on graphic design. Everyone at the tables was laughing and giggling. It felt like a conversation, not an interview.

I've shared similar stories with everyone I know and tell them part of my superpower is reading. When you read, you have the ability to connect with anyone about anything. The words on the pages of books and newspapers form intersections for people who come from different backgrounds, live in different parts of the country, or even have competing opinions. We can find something in common, even if that means you both read the same book or you have thoughts on how a reporter covered Michael Jordan's first retirement. It is a trick I have had to use time and time again. And it has worked each time.

I always have a book with me. Usually a paper-back is in my purse or work bag. It never fails that someone is going to ask me if it's a good read and from there we can start a conversation. As a trained reporter, I've used the trick a few times.

The first time was when I was a junior reporter playing out my internship in a very small south-ern town in Louisiana. My very first assignment was to write about the closing of a beloved local restaurant. I was sent there with little informa-tion. All I got was that a local restaurant was closing, the address and the name of the owner. I was supposed to come back with 1200 words ready to file for the next day's newspaper.

I used every tool in my tool box. First, I knew that if I could just get to the people, I would have all the answers. I drove around the neighborhood where the restaurant was located. I was looking for locals who could give me the rundown and details without adding the fluff. One quick pass along a few streets and I found a gas station that was home to a few local legends.

I could tell they were residents of the gas station because their setup was complete with a radio, several colored crates and both empty and full beer cans. These older white gentlemen had seen the world and experienced it. The stains on their overalls and the wrinkles in their hands held more stories than I could even imagine. They were at the point in their lives where they had forgotten more than I had learned. One had a long wooden stick hanging out the corner of his mouth and his partner in crime had a cigarette dangling from the tip of his finger. The ashes had burned down longer than the filter. These two were a sight.

I sashayed myself right up to them and smiled my biggest smile. Tool No. 2 — smile big. I told them that my assignment was to write a story about the restaurant, but I didn't know much. Tool No.3 — always tell the truth and ask the right question. I then explained that in Houston, my hometown, I knew that the generals on the corner held the keys to the city and knew everything. Tool No. 4 — flattery.

They looked at each other and started talking simultaneously. I had to slow them down so that I could capture it all. I wrote so much that I ran out of paper in my reporter's notebook and started writing on the back of receipts and random pieces of paper. While they were talking about the happenings of the city, I was able to talk about baseball and a few random facts about the city — all because of a book about sharecropping my dad gave me before I headed off for the internship. I recalled our exchange when he gave me the book. I was thinking out loud and said I am probably the youngest person to read this before throwing it in my suitcase. He said, "you never know when you will need it." Stay ready.

And here I was on the corner of a major intersection reciting facts like I was an encyclopedia and gathering facts like Sherlock Holmes. I turned in 1400 words that night and the story ended up on the front of the inside section, below the fold.

That wasn't bad for a young reporter from the big city.

The small piece of advice from my dad has played out so many other times in my life. I've learned to be prepared for anything and everything. There's a black jacket hanging in my office because I never know when I may end up in a business meeting that requires a jacket. I keep a pair of pearls in my office drawer just in case and 10 years ago — before children and the pandemic — I bought toilet paper and paper towels in bulk because you just never know when you might get stuck in the house.

Rather than trying to remember something or find something to write on, I walk around with a notebook. You can take notes, write down phone numbers and you have a place to refer to later. It has become a signature staple in my toolbox. I've got stacks and stacks of them in all colors and a few different sizes.

Late one Friday afternoon while working at the university, I was called to the president's office. His executive assistant mentioned that the president wanted to speak to me quickly. I rushed up and exchanged pleasantries and a few laughs before he motioned for me to sit down. Once I did, he just looked at me. It was uncomfortable for a few minutes before he finally asked if I was going to pull out my little notebook. I laughed and told him, I'd be right back. My little notebook had become synonymous with me being engaged and serious about the assignment or conversation. In his mind, I wasn't ready if I didn't have it.

That little notebook captured his ideas around a book list and how we would roll it out to the general public. He rattled off 20 or 30 books and authors and told me to make haste and get them ordered and reviewed. Before walking out the door, he gave me another piece of advice that has stuck with me. In fact, it changed my way of life and how I operate. He told me to order the books first and immediately because I would never know what was going to happen next. Essentially, do the work now so you don't have to do it later. I know there are life tips that tell you to do the hardest thing first to beat procrastination. I've also heard about eating dessert first and as a kid we did our homework and chores before playing, but his advice was different. He said point blank: Always do the things you know you have control over as soon as possible because something else is coming. You will need to be ready to do that then.

My colleagues and family members know if you ask me to do something, I am going to do it immediately if I can. I schedule meetings while in the meeting. I send the follow-up email as soon as I think about it. What I have learned is that too many things can get in the way of our best-made plans. If you don't do it now, you may not get to do it later.

Now reflecting on it, his advice seems more complicated than it had to be. But as a historical academician, he spoke in parables and added more words than were needed. Point blank he was telling me — stay ready so you don't have to get ready. Free your hands so you can use them when you need them.

It's a concept that many of us believe in. We want to be in the right place at the right time. We want to anticipate the next trends, but are we really ready? Have we done what is needed to take advantage of opportunity?

My best friend has hundreds of pictures with celebrities. I don't get it. She's like a magnet to opportunity. She's photographed with Marvin Sapp, Hillary Clinton, Mary J. Blige, Keith Sweat. You name them and in her house, there she is pictured right next to them. I didn't believe it until I experienced it myself. We were attending a concert following a HBCU classic football game. Sure, we had tickets that came with extra access but those did not guarantee access backstage or anywhere else. Wouldn't you know I looked up and there we were standing next to Reuben Studdard, "American Idol" Season 2 winner. How? We were in the right place at the right time. The crowd opened up and so did the gate. A friend ushered us through the security and boom we were there. We smiled as the cameras flashed. She whispered back to me and said, "you have to stay ready."

My mom worked for the airlines and as a result, I have flown standby my entire life. If you have ever flown standby, you are part of a select group of people who understand this level of stress. No matter how many times you look at the flight status or check the flight totals, the chance of getting one of those extra seats is always a toss-up that comes down to the last seven minutes before the flight is supposed to take off.

One weekend, I was headed home from a quick trip to see friends on the East Coast when I learned you have to be ready. I couldn't help staying a few extra hours for brunch, but I knew better than to pick a Sunday mid-day flight. It was something I had learned over time. Just as I knew no matter how many days I planned to be gone I needed to fly with only one piece of carry-on luggage, I knew it was better to fly out on the first flight, which people typically miss, creating an open seat. I've also learned (*I am sharing far too many secrets*) to walk up to the gate when you get there, let the agent know who you are and where you are on the standby list and sit within their eyesight.

There was absolutely no chance I was going to make this oversold flight. I was the fourth person on the list of standby passengers and there were zero seats available. It was the last flight out for the night and the forecast called for pretty bad weather in the next few hours. As boarding was winding down, my heart was racing and I was trying to figure out my next move. I didn't have a plan other than purchasing a ticket on another airline for an exorbitant amount of money and calling my friend to pick me up. Luck would have it that a delayed connecting flight would leave three seats available for standby.

Note: When you sit close to the counter, you hear everything that is going on via radio and the agents. The first name of the standby list was called. A husband and wife team. One seat left.

Two people in front of me. Their names were called. I began packing up my stuff and planning to head out. Then, my name was announced. I didn't ask questions and rolled right to the counter, scanned my ticket and walked down the jet way. What I learned was that the two before me needed to travel together, leaving me the next person up. Because I was ready to go, the counter agent moved me right on up. Stay ready.

I've learned to always be on my toes because of so many similar occasions and I've watched others miss their opportunity because they said they weren't ready. One random day, I got a phone call from a friend who needed a DJ for an event happening that day. It was an emergency, a Hail Mary of sorts but he was reaching out for anyone. In my phone, I have 12 different entries that have DJ in the contact name. I've met them at events or their contact information has been shared with me as a resource. I started calling and texting names down the list. The first six didn't answer or respond. The seventh did. He's now a regular working DJ for a national entertainment group that travels with comedians, musicians, speakers and athletes.

Two days after I reached out to those others, I started getting calls back. I told them what I was looking for and they said their ringer was off or they didn't have my number saved. Either way, they weren't ready and may have missed a-once-in-a-lifetime chance.

In everyday conversation, I've learned that you will meet someone who wants to be a singer, a teacher, something. Unfortunately, when you tell them you know someone or can help them pursue their goal, they will present you with a list of reasons why now isn't the time. It is unfortunate that many of us are waiting for the perfect time, when we are in the perfect shape and perfectly prepared for a dream we've defined. That's not how it works. We have to be ready to take advantage of what is in front of us. I've learned to answer my phone, respond to the text and be prepared to answer the request. You never know who you are sitting next to and who they know that could change your life.

Update your resumé, carry a business card, flush out your business plan and know what you need. Someone is going to ask you. Stay ready, so you don't have to get ready, is about remembering that everything can change in the blink of an eye and the plan we've laid out may need to be reworked for the current conditions. You have to be fluid and flexible, willing to change course.

In my city, there's the inner loop, the outer loop and now they've added an even bigger loop. Each of the tollways is designed to help those living in the suburbs have quicker and faster routes into the city. Wrong. These loops are crowded with suburbanites trying to make it into the city for work. At any point, a 20-minute commute can become an extended 45-minute drive because of a small accident or new road construction. You have to be willing to find an alternate route to get where you are going. You literally need to stay ready to change your plan and then possibly change it again.

There is a simple route from my home to my father's. You hop on one of the previously mentioned loops. Ride about 14 miles and exit. It's simple and straight to the point. I've driven that way to his house so many times, I can do it in my sleep. Of course, there are other ways to get there, but this is the easiest.

In 2021, when Houston was blacked out and frozen due to a failed electrical system, I found a new way to his house. After we all were left stranded at my home without electricity or a way to get warm, we packed up our cars to head for his house where there was a promise of lights. His neighbors had reported that they never went without electricity and the water was still on. We backed out the driveway cautiously and approached our route. What we found was pitch black stillness. There was not a streetlight, building light or anything for miles. There would be no way we could approach the tollway as the bridges were frozen over and public utilities had not made it out to clear or sand them down.

Without thinking, he headed down a residential street cut over to a minor thoroughfare and we followed that road for at least 10 miles before making a right and continuing down a similar road. In about an hour, we approached his neighborhood where there were lights and his neighbors welcomed us with a cookout of the items they saved from their refrigerator.

While I knew my dad knew a lot, I didn't expect that he knew how to travel across the city without ever entering a highway. After we settled in, he shared that while he had never taken that route he knew that he had to have a plan. He couldn't just turn around. He went to plan D — one he didn't know he even needed. *Stay ready.*

The Bottom Line.

The posture you should always have is preparation. Be prepared for whatever may be thrown at you and also for what you want and have been praying for.

A Little More.

You have heard that opportunity only knocks once. I'd challenge that notion and remix it to say opportunity knocks and then rings the doorbell of the person that is ready or the person that opens the door. If you miss it once, it's not coming back. But if you open the door and welcome the opportunity in, it will come back.

When you stand with your arms open and are ready to receive, you are in the position to always take advantage of an opportunity. This doesn't mean that you are perfect but it means that you are willing to be molded or pushed to go to the next level. You are prepared to execute on what you have. You are ready.

Your Turn.

- How many opportunities have you missed because you weren't prepared or paying attention?

- What will you do if you receive the things you weren't expecting?

- Are you ready to move from Plan A to Plan B without much work?

_____

_____

_____

_____

_____

_____

_____

_____

_____

_____

_____

_____

_____

_____

_____

_____

_____

_____

_____

_____

_____

_____

_____

_____

_____

_____

_____

_____

_____

_____

_____

_____

_____

_____

_____

_____

_____

_____

_____

_____

_____

_____

_____

Do You.

Big Pokey came to my birthday party. That may mean nothing to you if you aren't from the South. So let me explain. Big Pokey as in "Ball and Parlay" Pokey was at my house, sitting on my couch while we were celebrating my birthday. It was a big deal. To me. I mean, I do know all his verses on every song and I pretty much think that I could be a famous freestyle rapper based on listening to him throughout most of my teens and early 20s. As an original member of Houston's Screwed Up Click, his voice could be heard on most of the chopped and screwed songs. He equals some of the best parts of Houston.

In my eyes, he's the equivalent of a favorite childhood TV star or boy band singer. Just imagine if Rudy, from the Cosby Show, came to your house party. The probability of it happening is slim. But it happened to me.

And I was pumped. I live in a typical suburban neighborhood — a three bedroom, two bath house with an HOA and dog-friendly sidewalks. I drive an economical foreign car and work a 40-hour job, wear pearls and conservative heels to work most days and my life is probably more conservative than I'd care to admit.

My work wardrobe includes the standard Talbots, Chico's, Banana Republic and Ann Taylor pieces. I take my lunch most days and end almost all my emails with "cheers."

On my work commute, I blast gangsta rap, mostly Houston-based independent artists, but I am not afraid of 90s hip hop hits from Atlanta or Memphis. "Space Age Pimpin" by 8Ball and

MJG will forever be a classic. On the way home, I alternate between the local NPR station and gospel and I subscribe to several podcasts — "Ratchet and Respectable", "Code Switch", and "The Read". I have worked hard on my potty mouth and if left to my own devices I'd probably have five or so more tattoos than I currently have and I'd love to try blue hair.

Jazzercise, an aerobics-type class founded in 1968, is my little secret. I've dropped out a few times but keep going back. I'm often the youngest person and almost always the only Black person, but the camaraderie and interactions can't be beat. I convinced my best friend to attend a class with me. She thought it was a joke but once she joined, she quickly realized it was a full body workout that was fun and entertaining. She signed up immediately. I'll also take credit that she eventually became an instructor and later bought a franchise.

So while I was shocked that Pokey showed up at my house, I wasn't totally surprised. I've lived a life full of contradictions and surprises. I've come to find that the best parts of my life are at this very intersection. It's what makes my perspective mine.

If you looked at my resumé, you'd never guess that his visit was something that I will never forget. My credentials include me supporting executive leaders at some of the highest levels. I have represented organizations as the official spokesperson. I've harnessed national media attention and connected people and organizations that ultimately created business opportunities.

But what I look like or what I do isn't the full definition of me. I've said it before, don't let these pearls fool you. The attributes that make me aren't really Google-able.

The best parts of me are the experiences that have happened to me, the lessons I've learned along the way, the scars, and the success stories.

I refuse to miss out on the chance to meet someone new. To connect with a mind and talk about pop culture, compare notes on current events, or laugh at a local rapper. I can't just NOT offer suggestions on how to cope with a difficult situation or see my godson play t-ball. I am not going to miss the grand opening of a new hot spot, the opportunity to visit a new place, hear a live band, talk to my mentor about his childhood or celebrate with you. Do you expect me to pass up a good sale or not go to dinner with an old friend?

These are the ways I've learned to be me. It hasn't been easy. I've been shunned and criticized and questioned.

I witnessed a carjacking up close and personal. It was pretty scary, in fact. I was headed to the bank and was waiting for a parking spot when I noticed two people pushing and shoving. Before I knew it, a security officer was standing next to my car firing a gun in the direction of the altercation.

It was happening in slow motion. I saw the face of the security officer, watched him fire the gun and I followed the bullet with my eyes to the corner of the parking lot. I then watched the crook drive off and the old lady stood there as her car sped away. No one moved. I pulled my car into the spot and walked into the bank. All around me people were recanting the situation. Mostly adding their wrong but entertaining commentary. I called my boss and told her the story. She sent others over and helped me get home.

As a college student completing an internship away from home, I was afraid and a little shaken. My roommate and I stayed up much of the night talking and wondering what was going to happen. The police knocked on our door at 2:00 a.m. to show me a book of mug shots. Talk about being scared. I caught the next flight home.

My boss reached out when she learned I had left. After some discussion, she explained that the higher ups were surprised that I had left so abruptly. Their assumption was that because I was from the city and was Black, I'd seen something like this. I hadn't. True, I was Black. True, I was from what they considered a city. But carjacking, shooting and crime scenes are not what I had ever seen.

I was a girl from the suburbs who had the nickname Polo because I moved into a new neighborhood wearing argyle, pastels, K-Swiss and loafers while others were sporting Cross Colours and Dr. Martens. Carjacking was not what I knew.

That's the thing: you'd have no idea the life I've lived just by looking at me or even talking to me for a few minutes. And to be honest, most people are the same way. We are the sum of our parts and what you see is not the full story.

Once a coworker stared at me for a full five minutes during a random work day. She was studying my face, my eyes, my lips. Before moving to my clothes, she said she just didn't get me because I wasn't who she thought I'd be, for I knew a little bit about everything. Then, she laughed and said she liked it.

That was the start of our work-ship. She invited me to her family's house to play Loteria, we went antique shopping and she helped me select paint colors for my first house. We also went bowling, would hang out at the local bar and flirt with older men. As a result of stretching each other, our team blew sales goals out the water and our staff retention was revered.

That experience taught me that it was my job to bring my full self into a space. I couldn't hold back because I wanted to fit in or make others comfortable. That one coworker taught me that all of random facts I knew, and the stories I told, were of value. She told me that they made me a fuller person, better employee, better friend and leader.

It still took me a while to get this concept. The truth is that we are constantly in many transitional phases of our lives, often feeling lost and yearning to find the real version of ourselves. The one we feel comfortable sharing with others.

While I haven't figured it out, I can 100% say that when you are yourself, people can decide if you are someone that they can trust and follow.

If you are someone they should like.

This isn't easy as we have been conditioned to drown out what makes us who we are. We are told not to talk about the bad that has happened to us — our divorced parents, when we failed the test, that we aren't great at math or that we were addicted to drugs. This is especially the case for women and minorities in the workplace. We've been coached and forced into descriptors that help other people "swallow" us or accept us.

I can raise my hand and say I'm guilty. As I prepared to return to work after maternity leave, I came up with a list of things I wouldn't do. Talk about my kid was at the top of the list. I had drawn a line in the sand and declared I wouldn't share photos, bring his name up or talk about his sleeping habits.

I was so worried about how people would view me as a mom and as an employee. I had standard answers when people asked about him or my plans for school, sports, etc. I was back in the office for all of two days when I realized this wasn't going to work. I had run out of generic answers and people still had questions. They wanted to see pictures every day. I was truly interested in the life of others. And here they were, invested and interested in not just my child — but me as a mother. Quickly, I had to pivot back to home base. I am a natural sharer. I asked questions about others' kids and sent gifts for their birthdays and always bought the fundraiser items from my colleagues. What was I doing? I realized nope; this wasn't going to work. I wasn't being the real me.

Motherhood, the journey and the everyday challenges were part of me and primed me to be a better colleague and leader. This new role provided me with a new perspective. It was now part of my story.

I was able to share my thoughts on how the decisions we were making at the leadership table would impact parents. I shed light on how our policies and habits impacted working families.

My oldest son is famous in some rooms. He's loved by people he's never met. I'd also venture to say we've made some bold decisions as an organization because he was the face of a young Black boy, not just a data point. All because I decided to do me.

A few years ago I ran into a guy who was in college with me. He had such vivid memories of me from college. He was tickled that, according to him, I was exactly the same as he remembered. He said my pace of speech was the same, I laughed at the same jokes and had the same one-liners. He described me in ways I couldn't remember. He talked about how I worked hard, but was also at all the parties. He talked about how I had more than one pair of glasses and he remembered that I helped our class choose "Game Over" by Lil Flip to be our class song. In his words, I put Houston on the map. A quick Google search and you'll see that Lil Flip was a member of the Screwed Up Click just like Pokey.

I was intrigued by this because I had worked so

hard to remain myself since college. Over time, I had added therapy and was working hard to tone down my personality. I had been told I was a bit much and hard to handle. I was working through feedback I had received from a supervisor who said I was mean and too direct. An ex-boyfriend said I was high maintenance and extra and had a story for everything. And here was this guy, who was excited to tell me he was happy to see the me he remembered.

He was bragging to his wife that he remembered that I was confident and myself all the time. He encouraged us to be friends and was excited that we could connect.

Spoiler alert: All the therapy, executive coaching and counseling couldn't change me into someone else. You'd think I would have known this. I've taken probably 75 personality quizzes and no matter what happens, when I take them they ultimately give the same results (*ESTJ, My Enogram is 8, true color is orange*) over and over. They undermine his point that I was a true leader, I was a self starter, I was curious yet resolute, a quick learner and a people magnet.

He helped me to realize that I was always me and couldn't do anything about it. He simply said without even knowing, you can't run from who you are or what you have experienced. You are better when you are ... simply you.

The Bottom Line.

You have everything in you to be the best you. Your walk is your walk. Your experiences are your experiences. We are made up of our experiences and our race, sex, etc. Joseph Campbell said it best, "the privilege of a lifetime is to be who you are."

A Little More.

It is imperative to not get caught up in the game of comparison or the quest to get advice and input on every decision you make about your life. I heard this in passing, "don't consult with the people that don't have your gift." Everyone will have an idea, a perspective or a thought but not one of those people will have the full story, your complete perspective or your ability to be you. Your gift is yours and yours only.

Your Turn.

- When it's all said and done will you choose to do you?
- What does living boldly look like in your life?
- What's your gift?

———————————————————

———————————————————

———————————————————

———————————————————

———————————————————

———————————————————

———————————————————

———————————————————

———————————————————

———————————————————

———————————————————

———————————————————

———————————————————

———————————————————

———————————————————

———————————————————

———————————————————

———————————————————

———————————————————

———————————————————

You Only Have
One Mama.

No one really tells me I look like my mama. Most people say that I resemble my daddy and they usually say it with conviction, too. There's no possible way in their eyes that I could look like anyone else. His genes are pretty strong. The funny part of that is that I see my mom every time I look in the mirror. When I select my clothing or buy household items, she's the inspiration or guiding light. I can hear her voice when I say some words. I parent like her and I've got the pain in my left knee, just like her.

Despite these things, the truth is we are two very different women.

She's a bonafide brickhouse and, me, well just know we aren't built the same. She's got a round face that is full of love at all times and my long face doesn't always scream that I am friendly or even approachable. I have a pretty expensive taste and she always asks about the price of something before buying it. I can't sew, yet in her heyday she was whipping out outfits that would make Tim Gun from "Making the Cut" blush. Her whole house includes shades of soft gray and cleansing blue and my home's color scheme is "all the colors" — especially navy, emerald green and black and white. It works. I promise. She gives people a whole bunch of chances and I am using the three-strikes-and-you-are-out rule to govern my interactions.

Whether my mom and I look alike or have the same spending habits has nothing to do with our relationship. It is probably what draws us to each other. She is the ying to my yang. I call her at least once a day and if I see something I like, I will send it to her for approval and acknowledgment. I text her constantly and I buy two of everything — one for her and one for me. Everyone who knows me knows my mom. She comes up in my conversations with anyone and she knows all my secrets.

We've had some times of struggle like most mother-daughter combos. The disagreements are tied to disappointment and high expectations. There were a few years where we didn't talk. We existed around each other. There have been tense moments where we didn't support each other's decisions. It's a shocker, because as I said, mom is my person. But she raised me to be strong, independent and self-sufficient. Sometimes those attributes don't work well when you are being told what to do.

There's a poem that says you only have one mother. A mother that is kind and true. It goes on to say, when all others forsake you, she's right there for you. That's the truth. My mom has never left my side. During some of my hardest times, she is the center of my decision making. She reminds me of what I said I would do and keeps me honest to my own dreams and goals.

You won't even believe this, but both of my boys look just like her. I get so tickled when I see her facial expressions in their faces. One chews his tongue like her and the other hums the same way she does. All my friends said it as soon as they saw their first photos. It's like she had them herself. It's like God made sure I would always remember that she was integral to my motherhood journey.

I've always known that having a baby was going to be a challenge for me. I was never told by a doctor, but it has been somewhere in my thoughts, in my heart. When I played MASH, I didn't pay attention to the question about the number of kids. I don't know when I played with dolls and carried around a baby. I had a few names stored up but didn't practice saying them with my boyfriend's names. There were not a lot of babies around while I was growing up and the one that was born during my teenage years became my partner-in-crime for a few years. He grew up and left. I don't recall any hard feelings about it. It just was. As I reflect, I remember a few conversations about not having a motherly temperament. I think the jury was still out. Most people pegged me as someone who would focus on a career and not a family.

There were enough people I knew who had conceived very early in their life and had to make some tough choices as a result that kept me unworried about having a baby. I wasn't up for the work that seemed to come along with it. I knew others who couldn't seem to get pregnant (*not for lack of trying*) and a lot of my social circle just wasn't interested in being parents. Over time, I picked up the idea that babies would stop your life, pause your goals and tie you down. That was not what I was interested in. I wanted to live a life that included social activities, travel and fun. Nothing about adding a child seemed to match that.

So, after being married for five years and not being pregnant, I wasn't heartbroken. I assumed that it wasn't our time. We continued with living the "good life" — happy hours, clubs, vacations, concerts and fun. But as we got older and went out less, we started talking about family and began preparing and even practicing. It was light, nothing heavy. So, when we finally landed on the answer as to why we weren't getting pregnant after trying for a few years, I wasn't devastated. I was hurt and shocked, but not devastated.

We realized something wasn't adding up so we decided to talk to a doctor. During our first visit, an older white doctor who specializes in infertility took one look at me and decided I could not break down sugars and put me on a diabetes medication. He recommended surgery for my husband and told us to come back in six months. He talked fast and quickly. Moved us in and out of his office. There wasn't much question asking. We did everything he said and nothing happened.

We went back to him. Similar talking and diagnosing. Nothing happened.

Between work and life, we decided to take a break from trying to have a baby. We both threw ourselves into social activities. You saw us everywhere. We did everything but think about why we weren't having a baby. We threw parties, went on vacations, shopped, redecorated our house, and bought a new car. We did it all.

In the meantime, I read books, searched chat groups and started talking to a therapist about it. I needed to find balance and understand all the things that were happening. During the same period of time, my maternal grandmother was at her home recovering from a stroke. My mom and aunt had stretched their work time out and split the duties. It was the hardest three years of my life. I was watching my mother take care of her mother as she was fading away and I was taking care of my mother, as much as I could, while fighting to be a mother.

After a few months of avoidance, my husband and I had another discussion and decided to switch doctors. We showed up prepared with a long list of questions and a new approach. I also was set on us attending group counseling with others who were going through the same struggles. To me, we needed to be around others experiencing the same struggle. I remember the only session we attended. It was held in a small room and filled with middle-age white couples. There was not a single person of color and when we walked in everyone stared. We smiled and said our pleasantries.

There was a couple talking about their struggle with selecting a surrogate. Another couple got into a heated debate about selecting an egg donor. The wife brought up the idea that her husband could fall in love with the egg donor by looking at her photo and totally lose interest in her and ask for a divorce. At the same meeting, a couple shared how they were concerned they wouldn't love the child because they would know that the embryo was not made up of their cells. While I had mostly been quiet, their admission was a moment of clarity for me. I began tapping my husband on the leg and tapping my foot. A sign to him that I had something to say.

A declaration had come to me. I knew that no matter how we would have a child — adoption, IVF, IUI, surrogacy, sperm donation, whatever. There would be a baby in our home. I was clear that we would love the baby like it was our own. Too many Black families had gone before us and made a decision to raise a child and we were not going to be the people to decide that we could not love someone who may not be our blood offspring.

I couldn't hold back. I raised my hand and said to no one in particular what I knew. I shared that for years Black women had taken care of babies that weren't their own. They had been nannies and had mothered children that were left behind. They had served as the proxy for their cousins who couldn't care for a child. As teachers, nurses and neighbors, they had gone the extra mile. I explained that my husband's mother died when he was only five years old and his grandmother raised him and his brother after raising 16 of her own children. It was the first sign that we would be parents. I knew it.

Unfortunately, the doctor we were seeing didn't pan out; however, we got closer to the reason we weren't conceiving. We both went on diets and started a real journey to better health. It was difficult. Not only were we dealing with the devastating news (*and a reminder*) every day that we weren't having a baby naturally, we also had to stop eating out, staying up late, drinking, etc. and were on pretty tight regiments that included sleeping, working out and supplements. It was tough on our marriage. Our tempers were short, and frankly, we just didn't like each other. It was hard to explain everything that was happening to our family and friends and it was one of the loneliest times of my life.

My mom once told me something along the lines of she wishes she could be like me. Something about how I just make a decision and do it. She wrote me a letter that detailed it out. She all but said I was stubborn and she loved me for it.

She never quite understood the fertility journey. The truth is no one could. It was hard to explain and once I started talking about it, I would get frustrated and change the subject. But she was there along the way, loving me through every single step.

She would, in her own way, check on us when we started progesterone shots. She always found a way to tell one of us that she cooked something. She didn't ask much about the process of shots. She hated that we needed help to conceive but she knew exactly what time we had to take shots and she called just to ask what was on TV, or what we were eating. Her secret way of making sure we were doing what we were supposed to be doing.

Throughout our entire journey, I knew that I would not conceive until my mother was able to focus on being my mother. It was the strangest thing to know, but just as clear as day I knew it.

She knew it too.

In June 2018, my grandmother took her final breath. I was there with my mother when it happened. It was uneventful. She and I went into our rhythm. I checked on her and made the appropriate phone calls to the pastor, friends and family and whatever else, while she went into action taking care of the details.

At the funeral, I sat next to mama. I held her hand and made sure no one bothered her. The ceremony went well and it was good to see all mama's friends. One by one, they whispered to me how they were proud of my mama for being so strong. Others shared how she helped them through their hard times with her kind words and words of wisdom. Mama has always had a word for someone.

And without knowing it, I've picked up that trait — mothering. Even though I hadn't conceived yet, I still managed to be motherly to others. I've answered the call of so many who have asked that I mentor them. I followed a young lady on Twitter and based on her posts, I could see that she and I were aligned and shared some similar life struggles. We met up for lunch and before it was over, I was giving her advice on her job hunt. I specifically went there hoping to get advice from her.

Mom didn't know that we had decided to try one last time with a new doctor. Our appointment was set for August. If you like a good story, you know that we walked into this doctor's office, she took one look at our paperwork, our numbers and said that our case would be easy. We began fertility treatments immediately. There were no delays and everything went smoothly. I have to believe grandmother approved of the process and ensured it all went the way it was supposed to go.

It was truly a blessing. The timing couldn't have been better. Mom retired and was able to grieve while also celebrating her first child carrying her first grandchild. Once I told her officially that I was pregnant, she became a new person. She started redecorating her house. She had questions about who was going to be in the room when I delivered and she planned a shower for her friends. She cleaned our refrigerator and bought clothes for the unborn baby. She turned into a whole new person.

We had huge and long discussions about her moving in. She didn't want to give up her independence but wanted to be in the decision-making process of what was happening at my house. Our final agreement was that she would stay during the week at my house and return to her home on the weekends. She did that for a year and a half. The time was only extended because of COVID.

Her being at our house helped in so many ways. I was able to transition back to work. We had food cooked when we came home and our son received an overwhelmingly loving start to learning. His first word was book, but Mimi wasn't too far behind. To this day, life is better when Mimi pops up and stops over. She brings with her an aura that's calming and reassuring. She's a bit firm but also gentle.

It's not lost on me that my dreams only come true because of the sacrifices she made. The overtime she passed up to take me to practice or the happy hour with friends she missed so she could find whatever new thing I was doing. My dreams are still coming true because she's Mimi.

The Bottom Line.

The journey to motherhood looks different for everyone. It doesn't always happen the way the nursery rhyme says, "first comes love, then comes marriage, and then comes the baby in the baby carriage." The order could be different. The carriage may show up as something else.

Your Turn.

- In what ways are you expecting your life to be like the nursery rhymes?
- When life doesn't present itself exactly that way, how are you reacting?
- What is happening while you wait for your fairytale ending?

_____

_____

_____

_____

_____

_____

_____

_____

_____

_____

_____

_____

_____

_____

_____

_____

_____

_____

_____

_____

_____

_____

_____

_____

_____

_____

_____

_____

_____

_____

_____

_____

_____

_____

_____

_____

_____

_____

_____

_____

_____

I Am Rich.

I've had enough leadership training to last me nearly a lifetime. While that may sound like a complaint, it's not. I am always eager to learn something new about myself, reflect on my actions, and the root causes of my reactions. I am totally into continuous improvement of myself.

While most people dread their performance evaluations, I am eager to use the time to be reflective and considerate of my goals and how close or far I am from reaching them. Franklin Covey's "Seven Habits of Effective People" is alarmingly interesting to me. While I have veered away from the full system, his habit — begin with the end in mind— is how I function. I've got a goal and about two to three plans to get there. His description of the habit is where it really gets deep. Begin With the End in Mind means to begin each day, task, or project with a clear vision of your desired direction and destination, and then continue by flexing your proactive muscles to make things happen.

I've taken those directions to heart. I am eager to get better and to get there faster. I'm open to learning new ways to approach leadership, balancing life and reading and hearing about how others have done it and thrived.

In a most recent leadership course, we were focusing on what our stand in life was. We went around the room trying to articulate what our individual stands could be. I remember a classmate who mentioned her relationship with her granddaughter and how her stand was to be 100% present whenever they were together. I

couldn't help but to believe that it was such a no-
ble and sweet choice for a relationship that was
precious and important. A male executive spoke
about honoring the voice of others when making decisions. He based his choice on feedback
he received after a female employee complained
about several of his organization's practices and
policies.

Their decisions seemed so thoughtful. As my
turn approached, I had no clue as to what I
would say. I considered my relationships to be
personal and professional, I thought about how
I treated others and how I was going to pursue
my goals. While there were areas on that list that
I wanted to improve and relationships that could
be better, nothing stood out as a point of action
to take a bold hard line for.

The facilitator approached me as she walked
around the room talking to participants about
the assignment. She could see I was working and
hadn't yet landed on anything. As a way of building conversation and triggering the students at
the table with me, she asked what would be our
wish if we only had one.

I was thinking, now lady I couldn't answer the
first question, how do you expect me to answer
this? My partner blurted out, I'd want to be rich.
The rest of the table chimed in with head nods
and loud yeses. I shrugged my shoulders. They
questioned me, who doesn't want to be rich?

Me: I'm already rich.

I think everything that happened next, happened in slow motion. People from across the room looked at me with googling eyes, those close to me examined my shoes, purse, jewelry, and clothes. I could imagine they were trying to see how "rich." I really was.

Me again: I'm rich. I'm rich in love, hope, and family. I'm rich in experience, in joy and in adventure. I'm rich in friendship, in mercy, in grace. I'm rich in confidence and laughter.

And I meant every single word of it.

I've known this my entire life. And if you ask my mom, my requests as a small child reflect my champagne taste. I partially blame it on my grandmother who dressed me up in ruffled dresses, matching socks and white patent leather shoes and paraded me to all the flea markets on the hunt for antiques.

While she worked hard for every dollar, she used it to fund her extravagant taste and fanciful life. That manifested in an oversized gold leaf painted dresser with a thick slab of heavy veined marble that was topped by four trays of beautiful perfume bottles. The kind of bottles you buy at the store and vintage atomizers with pumps and silk tassels. You could also see her affinity for nice things with the brocade fabric curtains and the ever changing furniture and porcelain knick knacks.

Ruby Lee didn't play. She went to the beauty shop every Saturday, carried designer bags and wore only the best J. Renee shoes and Casper suits to church. She exuded luxury and opulence. Her yard was immaculately groomed and filled with beautiful flowers and stark white monuments.

She set the tone for how she would be treated and helped me to imagine a perspective that has me believing — even today — that I can have anything I want. She made it clear to me and so many others that everything is attainable. Because of her, I know I belong in every space I enter and nothing is off limits.

I have very vivid memories of her house. In fact, many of her furniture pieces have made their way to my home. It smelled like extravagance and was always filled with love. Those are the memories that hug me when I think about her. The feeling of love that she put in the air, the aura of confidence that she embedded in her life, and the prayers of hope and mercy are what remind me that you aren't valuable because of your valuables. They are the icing on the cake. Your heart is what makes you rich.

Once I learned her story (*as a child, I just knew she was my grandmother, I didn't know the details of how she was able to be fancy*) and how she worked very hard, including having multiple jobs, running several businesses while managing a household, being active in her community, serving her church and supporting her growing family. She did it all with her own hands and the resources she had. Her approach was that she had everything she needed within her.

As a result, I walk around believing that I want for nothing. She helped me to see that I already have what I need. I am rich.

I've kept the notion that when your hands are open because you are giving, you can't help but receive something. Time and time again this has proven true. I don't know where I picked this up but if someone compliments my costume jewelry, I take it off and give it to them. When it happens the receiver is usually surprised or taken aback. And I tell them don't worry about me because the story goes that because I have given to them, I will get double. It has worked every single time. My jewelry collection is more than I can wear and dream of wearing.

Recently, I watched, my hands being filled in the form of baby formula. Within two days of having a baby, our chosen formula was recalled. That recall sent the formula industry into a tailspin, ultimately breaking the supply chain. I will forever count it as one of the scariest times of my life. How in the world do you feed an infant without baby formula?

With breastfeeding off the list of options, we were close to relying on the old-school remedies of boiled milk. Unfortunately, the doctor's office couldn't assist as manufacturers simply could not produce enough inventory. Add in a baby with a severe cow's milk allergy and you can never imagine the pressure a mom like me was feeling while balancing all the feels that go along with postpartum, managing a toddler and returning to work. While I was stressed, I never doubted that baby brother would have food. Count it faith or mother's intuition, I knew it would come together.

While ending my second week back to work after maternity leave, my boss casually asked if I was dealing with the baby formula shortage. The story had not made its way to the top of the news cycle and without having friends or family fighting for formula, many people just weren't aware.

It was an honest question, but she had no idea of my response and how it would trigger. Through quick tears, I explained how we were on our fifth brand of formula and were having a hard time securing additional cans of the only formula he could digest. I told her about the secret web of mamas across the country who were purchasing milk in our local stores and shipping it to moms who wouldn't find it in their neck of the woods. We had worked out a system, unfortunately, the formula we needed was hard to find.

Of course, she offered her concern and acknowledged the frustration. Within minutes, I received several notifications. Her friends were responding to a post she made about my situation. Before the end of the week, a young lady drove more than 200 miles to deliver 16 cans of baby formula to me. She had collected them from stores in her area of the state. She wanted nothing in return and to this day, her family and I stay connected. I've heard the promise so many times and there's a particular sermon I heard in 2019 where our deacon of finance plainly said these two things: If people have a genuine need, you are supposed to help them AND if you don't give, you are saying you don't trust God AND you don't fear him.

Both of those reminders of promise showed up.

As I said, I am rich. I have resources, connections, people who care about me and a village of support. Rich.

What I have also learned is that being rich is a mindset. You become rich in your mind before you become rich in your bank account. That currently comes in the form of life experiences — hard days and long nights. It comes from asking questions and challenging assumptions. It comes from developing a stand that you have everything you need even before you need it.

The Bottom Line.

We are all rich and have everything we need.

A Little More.

My phone is filled with screenshots, quotes, memes and Bible study notes. My friend always, always has a pondering that makes sense. Herbert said, "The toughest issue for lottery winners is that many of them try to live a regular life after winning. Rich folk do not live like us regular folk. Everything has to change or you'll fail. NOTHING will be the same."

Your Turn.

- Now that you know you are rich, what are you going to do differently?

_____

_____

_____

_____

_____

_____

_____

_____

_____

_____

_____

_____

_____

_____

_____

_____

_____

_____

_____

_____

_____

_____

_____

_____

_____

_____

_____

_____

_____

_____

_____

_____

_____

_____

_____

_____

_____

_____

_____

_____

_____

_____

_____

_____

_____

_____

_____

_____

_____

_____

_____

_____

_____

_____

_____

_____

_____

_____

_____

_____

_____

Shine.

I had the honor of addressing my sorority sisters during the 100-year anniversary of the founding of our organization. It was a surprise request and an honor I didn't take lightly. I tried for weeks to develop the speech that accompanied the mood — a Black Greek letter organization grounded in service and sisterhood was celebrating what our founders accomplished in 1920. At the same time, while financially active, I wasn't moving my feet and serving the way I should.

The event was open to the public and once I told a few people, they were excited to be there. Many of them were professional women who were balancing love, life, kids and family. I knew the message had to be able to reach them in all parts of their life. I listened to Oprah's commencement speeches from previous years for inspiration. My favorite is still her remarks to the 2012 class at Spelman, where she reminded students that they needed to know who they are, that service and significance equal success and that doing the right thing is always the best choice. She will forever be my favorite orator, writer and tastemaker. She has the ability to be herself and share things with just the right tone and cadence. She can connect with anyone yet will always be herself no matter what.

Before many big events, I often channel her and remind myself just to be me. Like her, I try to move out of the way and let the words come out and sit with the person who needs to hear it. Sometimes, I pick my glasses based on her latest pair and I've been known to even use her as a style muse.

The concept of "Do You." came from a presentation I gave on personal branding. I asked participants to think of a person — a celebrity — who had a brand and to describe it in just a few ways.

A few people mentioned Drake, who happened to be the hottest artist of the time. I heard Michael Jordan was being considered as the GOAT (*Greatest Of All Time*). I'd bet if I asked now, we'd hear about Donald Trump, Deion Sanders and maybe even Kanye West.

No matter when asked, the best example of a personal brand is Oprah. She has found a way to be a tastemaker (*Oprah's Favorite Things List*), a promoter of others (*Oprah's Book Club*) and entrepreneur (*HARPO*). We also can't forget she's got her own magazine and has been on the cover of every issue.

Those are some of the very things that I hope resonates with others when they think about me. It's a high bar, but I set it every single time. The keynote address was no different.

My remarks were long, but here's part of what I said:

This, my sisters, is the time to shine your light and shine it brightly. It is time that people recognize you and all that you bring to the table, not only in terms of our sisterhood, but in your daily lives. We must all shine brightly.

It's no secret. As women, we have it hard. Tremendously hard. It's not fair. It's not right. It's not cool. But, it's true. Every day, we're called to bear the heavy loads, have all the answers and that means accepting less for ourselves all while giving the most of ourselves to everyone who "needs" it.

So many of us are the CEOs of our household, the maids, the chefs, the Uber, the nurse, the counselor, therapist and the medic. We are like air traffic controllers directing what's coming in and what's going out. And to top it all off... women outlive men in almost every society. In more developed countries, the average life expectancy at birth is 79 years for women, 72 years for men.

Y'all... women are making it happen. We've heard about the "hidden figures," we read how much our First Lady Michelle Obama endured and the Queen Bee Beyoncé has described some of her own life's challenges in her work. Without a doubt, all that stuff, all the stuff we are dealing with leads to that bright light we all have dimming just a little bit.

If we're honest, every day we aren't walking around as our best self. We're feeling insecure and less than tired and empty. Doesn't matter how much we're working out, meditating or relaxing at night, it's a lot. Here's the challenge I offer — this is not the time to dim our light.

There's a lot at stake and each one of us has a light that matters. It is incumbent upon each of us to let our light shine brightly and let it fuel us to even higher heights of greatness. Our families are depending on us. Our friends are depending on us. One would say the nation is depending on us. Now is not the time to dim our light.

*Our insecurities around our self-promotion, cre-
dentials, and contributions will disappear when
we understand that the stakes for us to succeed are
so high that we are almost forced to tell our story
for the sake of being a resource to someone else. We
have an important story that needs to be told and
heard. Now is not the time to dim our light.*

When I picked the word shine as my mantra in
2016, I did so not knowing how much it would
resonate with others or how it would take off. I
simply chose it as a reminder to me. It's simple.

To shine, you:

- Do your best at all times.

- Do everything with excellence.

- Come to the table prepared.

- Look the part, act the part.

- Bring it all and bring it in a way that makes
  people know who you are.

- Put your best foot forward.

For me, shining is showing up as being the best
version of myself. Being positive when things
look bad. Finding ways to bring light to dark
situations and speaking things as they are

Long before it became my theme for the year,
one of my supervisors noticed it. Thinking back,
I was myself the entire time I was there. The environment was conducive to us being creative
and competitive. We played games at work, went
on field trips and had dress up days. But it was

also hard work; we were always upping our sales goals. Because I didn't go to an Ivy League school like my colleagues, I never thought I quite fit in. On her last day, she bought us all gifts. She presented me with a business card holder that was covered in rhinestones. I smiled politely and tucked it away. I figured it was a good standard gift for a young professional. It wasn't until a few months later when I came across it again, that I found the inscription: never stop shining. That was 2002, I now have shirts, journals and coffee mugs to remind me about my little light. I've been tagged on social media, shouted out on graduation announcements and have art that has shine mentioned. It has become a personal mantra, a way of life. So it felt right to bring it to this audience.

After the event was over, I received a few comments from those who were in the room about how glad they were to be reminded about the importance of their light. Someone else told me they felt like I gave them permission to be themselves.

For a brief moment, I felt how Oprah must have felt when she taped a great show. I was simply being me. In that same commencement speech to Spelman grads, she brings up that fact that people would call her a brand and she'd say... I'm just being me.

That to me is it! I'm not doing anything special or outrageous. And if that's what shining is, well then, I'm just gonna shine.

The concept of shining is even in the Bible.

Matthew 5 says "Let your light so shine before men, that they may see your good works, and glorify your Father which is in heaven."

And over in John, the Bible teaches: "The light shines in the darkness, and the darkness has not overcome it."

Both are reminders that light prevails. It can't be ignored. Whether you follow the teaching of God or not, I can guess that you've experienced someone who has walked into a room and caught your attention. You've remembered their smile or something about them drew to you. That's their light. That's their shine.

At the university, we hosted monthly events that brought in speakers from across the country. The speakers ranged from big-time motivational speakers to local social justice activists. This particular year, student leaders had convinced us to bring in ET — Eric Thomas. Thomas was all over social media and had become famous for his memorable line: "When you want to succeed as bad as you wanna breathe then you will be successful."

I had purchased his book and was ready for the night. It was a packed house full of students, athletes, employees and others eager to hear ET's one-liners. After checking on the speaker room, I ran into this kid. He caught my eye from across the auditorium. Something was drawing me to him. He wasn't the main speaker, and wasn't really connected to the speaker's entourage. He didn't have on a suit or fancy clothes. He was just around and I couldn't help but notice him.

If I'm honest he had a light or an aura.

I was the little kid who touched everything hot. The brighter it was, the more intrigued I was by it. I've heard more than a few stories about me sticking my finger in a candle or putting something in the electrical outlet. Lucky for me, there is no permanent damage.

I was drawn to the light of this young man and needed to know who he was. I walked right up to him. I introduced myself and learned that he was assigned to come and advance for the speaker. He told me his name was Tobe. No last name, but suave in his response. He had a presence. Everything about his response was cocky. Had an attitude for no reason and was kind of aggressive. I bet I asked him who he was supposed to be. He told me he was going to be famous. I said, bet. He came back and said if I ever needed anything to call him. His number is still in my phone right now.

Well now, guess what? He's famous. World famous. All because he was who he said he was.

Some people water down themselves to blend in. He was shining and had no intention of fitting in.

You too have it. It's all over you. You just have to have the audacity to stand out. To stop shrinking. It's easier said than done. Trust me, I'm telling you what I know, not what I heard.

I've been told, more than once, that I do the most. Sometimes, I receive it as a critique. Other times, I take it as a compliment. Being this way has gotten me through life with joy and excitement. Doing the most makes me a good storyteller, keeps me grounded and connected to others. It also keeps me out of trouble. When you are doing the most, you don't have time to make mistakes and waddle in them. Instead, you are too busy planning your next move or recovering from the last one.

I was given an assignment. You know the 20% of your job description that's other duties as assigned? This fell dead into that category. The task connected me with an older woman. She had broken barriers in her career, then took a role at her local university. During our call, she gave me a lot of things to do. As a side bar: this always happens to me. I'm assigned the person who has been the most difficult, the most demanding and the person adopts me and begins pouring into me. The person stays in touch and has a true interest in my well being. But I digress, back to the story. She has been retired for about 25 years. During her retirement she was leading her sorority, heading up several organizations at church and attending all city councils meetings as a watchdog. As she was giving me orders, she dropped a jewel: If You Want Something Done, Ask a Busy Person To Do It. She described me to a tee.

Doing the most really isn't about me. I figured that out recently. Doing the most is about using all 24 hours of a day to be a blessing. To be an example. To be a connector. I bring it all to the table. That's what I figured out. I couldn't define it exactly. And I tried. And somehow a definition hit me in the forehead.

It's the bullet points I listed above, it's standing out in the crowd, it's bright eyes and a great smile. It's what Oprah said — doing your best at all times even when people aren't looking — and it's having the audacity to be your damn self and then understanding that even then, you need to continue getting better.

You get to figure out what shining means to you. Whatever you come up with, do it. And do it all the time. Don't worry about what other people think or if you have to ask someone to help you craft a perfect definition. Don't worry about outshining anyone, just shine. Make sure your light is shining bright for those who need us to light the way for them and be prepared to find the people who will do the same when your time comes.

The Bottom Line.

When God said, "let there be light," he gave you permission to shine. It is our job to light the way for others. People are watching you and God has given you the ability to be a light in a dark world.

Your Turn.

- How are you shining your light?

_____

_____

_____

_____

_____

_____

_____

_____

_____

_____

_____

_____

_____

_____

_____

_____

_____

_____

_____

_____

_____

_____

_____

_____

_____

_____

_____

_____

_____

_____

_____

_____

_____

_____

_____

_____

_____

_____

_____

About The Author.

Sheleah D. Reed has been called a "shero" by some people—but really, she just calls herself honest. She is a connector of people, an identity coach, and an unapologetic believer in the power of audacity.

Sheleah's confidence and authenticity are contagious, empowering others around her to embrace their own uniqueness. Her life's work focuses on helping people find their purpose through self-discovery and bringing their authentic selves to the forefront in their careers, relationships and personal lives.

As someone who looks for lessons in every moment, she wrote *Do You. The Audacity to Live a Bold and Authentic Life* to help others discover who they really are by sharing her own experiences — experiences that helped her figure out how to live boldly and unapologetically.

By day, she is a leader among leaders in her dual role as chief of staff and chief communications officer of a large urban school district. She is known for her unique style and discerning perspective. But the qualities that make Sheleah who she is can't be found on Google.

She enjoys collecting antiques, yet is a sneaker admirer (especially of bright colorways). As a native Houstonian, she can recite ANY Houston hip hop lyric, yet dances like nobody's watching at Jazzercise classes. Some may call it a contradiction, but she thrives at intersections.

Ultimately, she believes God is always in control, is not afraid to speak her mind, and loves reading. Her husband is her partner in power and they have two sons who are the best gifts they could ever have received.